Advance I
for
D0005812

Confessions of a
Part-Time Sorceress

A GIRL'S GUIDE TO THE DUNGEONS & DRAGONS® GAME

"Who says boys should have all the fun? Not Shelly Mazzanoble, anyway. With good humor and a swing or two of her mace, she advances fearlessly on the mostly male bastion of Dungeons & Dragons and comes through it with nary a scratch on her. For the girl gamer who's been itching to slay ogres with the best of 'em, this is the book for you."

—Peter Archer, author of *The Great White Wyrm*

"Shelly Mazzanoble gives D&D the make-over it deserves—watch out Tyra!"

—J. Marin Younker, Librarian, Seattle Public Library

"Fresh, funny, and smart. I was expecting [the book] to be informative, but I wasn't expecting it to be so very entertaining. The next time I meet a woman that I think might be interested in playing D&D, I'm going to give her a copy of this book before I do anything else. It really covers all the bases and introduces the game with a perspective that is fun and unique, but still completely accurate and helpful."

—Monte Cook, game designer

"I had some gamer friends over the other day flipping through the [book], and they were all laughing their heads off. My husband and I have also enjoyed reading bits of it out loud to each other. . . . ."

—Spring Lea Henry, library consultant and former editor of YAttitudes, ALA's journal for YA librarians

"This book is one of the best introductions for D&D I have ever read. It conveys not just the feel of the game, and why every sensible female of any species should play it, but it's FUN! A cool, hip, and cutting-edge welcome mat for the game."

—Ed Greenwood, creator of *The Forgotten Realms* and acclaimed fantasy author

Confessions of a Part-Time Sorceress

A GIRL'S GUIDE TO THE DUNGEONS & DRAGONS® GAME

By

Shelly Mazzanoble

Introduction by

R.A. Salvatore and Diane Salvatore

Confessions of a Part-time Sorceress:
A Girl's Guide to the DUNGEONS & DRAGONS® Game

©2007 Wizards of the Coast, Inc.

This book is protected under the copyright laws of the United States of America. Any reproduction or unauthorized use of the material or artwork contained herein is prohibited without the express written permission of Wizards of the Coast, Inc.

Published by Wizards of the Coast, Inc. Wizards of the Coast, DUNGEONS & DRAGONS and their respective logos are trademarks of Wizards of the Coast, Inc., in the U.S.A. and other countries.

All Wizards of the Coast characters, character names, and the distinctive likenesses thereof are property of Wizards of the Coast, Inc.

Printed in the U.S.A.

The sale of this book without its cover has not been authorized by the publisher. If you purchased this book without a cover, you should be aware that neither the author nor the publisher has received payment for this stripped book.

Editors: Michele Carter with Nina Hess

Cover and Interior Illustrations: Craig Phillips

Cover and Graphic Designer: Karin Powell

First Printing: September 2007

9 8 7 6 5 4 3 2 1
ISBN: 978-0-7869-4726-3
620-21540740-001-EN

Library of Congress Cataloging-in-Publication Data

Mazzanoble, Shelly, 1972-
    Confessions of a Part-time Sorceress: A Girl's Guide to the Dungeons & Dragons Game /
by Shelly Mazzanoble.
        p. cm.
    ISBN 978-0-7869-4726-3
    1. Dungeons & Dragons (Game)—Humor. 2. Dungeons & Dragons
(Game)—Social Aspects—Humor. 3. Women Fantasy Gamers—Humor. I.
Title.
    GV1469.62.D84M39 2007
    793.93—dc22

                                                                    2007014685

U.S., CANADA,	EUROPEAN HEADQUARTERS	Wizards of the Coast,
ASIA, PACIFIC, & LATIN AMERICA	Hasbro UK Ltd	Belgium
Wizards of the Coast, Inc.	Caswell Way	't Hofveld 6D
P.O. Box 707	Newport, Gwent NP9 0YH	1702 Groot-Bijgaarden
Renton, WA 98057-0707	GREAT BRITAIN	Belgium
+1-800-324-6496	Save this address for your records.	+32 2 467 3360

Visit our Web site at www.wizards.com

For Mom, Dad 'n Mike

Table of Contents

Chapter One
Babes in Boyland 1
The Geek Factor — 8
You Might Be a Roleplayer If . . . — 14
DUNGEONS 'n DRAGONS Rulz! — 20

Chapter Two
Building Character 31
But She Has a Pretty Face — 33
Check Yourself Before You Wreck Yourself — 37
Finding My Inner Elf — 39
Racial Profiling — 40
Have Some Class — 41
Group Therapy — 47
Are You a Good Witch or a Bad Witch? — 48
Baby's Got Back . . . Story — 52
Game On! — 54

Chapter Three
Will Work for Masterwork Armor 61
Gold Digging — 62
Does This Chainmail Make Me Look Fat? — 64
Weapon of Choice — 66
Lotions and Potions and Plasma Screen TVs — 70
Uh Oh, It's Magic — 72
Spelling Under the Influence — 75
You Cast a Spell on Me — 77
How to Spell Pizzazz — 78

Table of Contents

Chapter Four
Love is a Battlefield..............85
Basic Training — 88
Hit Me with Your Best Shot — 90
Doing Unto Others As They Can Do Unto You — 91
Dungeon Tours Begin at 3:00 — 94
The Etiquette of War — 94
Dungeon Decorum — 106
The Penguin Cometh — 109

Chapter Five
Where's the Party? 117
Members Only — 120
Mastering Your Domain — 121
Master Class — 124
Storming Your Castle — 125
Drunkards and Dragons — 127
Death Becomes Her — 148
Love is in the Air — 157

Appendix......................165
Cheaters Never (well, hardly ever) Win — 165
Designing Women — 166
Word Up — 173
Endgame — 179
Acknowledgments — 181

Introduction (Hers)

I really want to play the D&D game. I have never said that before, although as you could likely guess, I know more avid gamers than the average woman. I am literally surrounded by them.

My husband, both of my sons, and even most of my nephews spend a great deal of time rolling dice. And discussing their great adventures in detail. I have spent countless hours listening to the stories of gamers.

The men in my life are predominantly gamers, and the only thing gamers love to do more than play the games is tell the stories of the games they have played. Some of the stories they tell repeatedly. They are like fishing tales or golf stories; they get bigger, and better, over the years.

Don't believe me? Ask my husband to tell you the wubbah wubbah story. He will, and you'll laugh, trust me. I have only been tempted to play once, years ago when the kids were starting to get into D&D.

And now I am tempted to play D&D once again. Shelly's style is so entertaining and easy to read that she has inspired me to try again. She breaks it down in such a way that I actually understand the lingo, an amazing feat when you consider how little I actually understood after all these years of listening to "the Guys'" crazy adventures.

—*Diane Salvatore*

Introduction (His)

There is no better way to describe a conversational game like D&D than with a conversational style. Shelly didn't "write a book" here as much as she engaged in a fun conversation. Hey, it's D&D, and as my wife just pointed out, anecdotes not only matter, they ARE the point of it all!

I wish I had found this book in 1980, when I started playing (Shelly was probably a baby, then). One of the things that irked me in my early days of D&D (my college days) was that we couldn't get the girls to join in. That was true when I was single, and even more true after I met Diane—I really wanted her to share this part of my life with me. But it was intimidating to her. D&D books were written by gamers, who, for the most part in 1980, were guys. So thank you, Shelly, for bridging the communication gap, and to all you younger D&D guys out there, get this book and bring on the girls. And for all you girls out there wondering what the heck this "gaming" thing is all about, here's your answer—and a ticket to a heck of a lot of fun.

—R.A. Salvatore

TOP 10 MYTHS ABOUT DUNGEONS & DRAGONS

1. You need to speak with a British accent when playing

2. You have to play in a dark, dank basement in the home of someone's mother

3. You need to drink full-sugar soda and eat chips that stain your fingers orange

4. No one cool plays (or has ever played) *DUNGEONS & DRAGONS*

5. No one you know has played (or still plays) *DUNGEONS & DRAGONS*

6. It will take you the rest of your natural life to learn the rules

7. If you start playing *DUNGEONS & DRAGONS*, your friends will abandon you and your subscription to **match.com** will mysteriously be deactivated

8. The game involves boards, incense, finger pricks, solemn oaths, sacrifices, or hazing rituals

9. You will start dressing like a musical theater major and insist on wearing leotards, capes, or turtlenecks

10. You will develop an insatiable urge to attend Renaissance festivals

Fireball: Turn asses to ashes

Chapter One
BABES IN BOYLAND

Let me just lay it out here: I am a girly girl.

I get pedicures, facials, and microderm abrasions. I own more flavors of body lotions, scrubs, and rubs than Baskin Robbins could dream of putting in a cone. I organize my shoes by heel height, sort my handbags by strap length, and store my nail polish on the butter shelf of my refrigerator. I shop, watch soaps, and religiously dish on the fashion choices and bad judgment of whomever *Us Weekly* deems the most newsworthy. I not only embrace my inner girl, I full on squeeze the stuffing out of her.

I am also an ass-kicking, spell-chucking, staff-wielding 134 year-old elf sorceress named Astrid Bellagio. At least, I am once a week when I play DUNGEONS & DRAGONS.

Let's not get carried away here. I wasn't always a gamer. Until recently my escapades involving anything with dice, boards, and little primary colored markers were limited to *Chutes and Ladders*, *Sorry!*, or a warm keg of beer and a red plastic cup.

I have those friends who are *very* into games, mainly the computer or video game variety. Heard the one about the guy who turned down tickets to a U2 concert because it was the same night that his *World of Warcraft* guild held strategy council meetings to plan for Saturday's raid? Yeah, I know him. In fact, I dated him for two years. He was smart, charming, compassionate, and good-looking. He was also a level fifty-four gnome warrior named Aggro. We broke up shortly after he answered my panicked phone call from the shoulder of I-5 during rush hour with, "I can't talk now! I'm fighting the end-level boss in the Zul'Gurub raid!" Well screw you, Zul'Gurub and the end-level boss! His girlfriend was stranded on the side of one of the country's most congested freeways with a flat tire. Not to mention I was wearing white pants that day.

The reason I never got into games is simple: I'm not competitive. It's also why I never kicked Cindy Bleecher's ass for making out with Kyle Pinter in eighth grade even though she *knew* I liked him. More significantly, right around the time Grandma and Grandpa gave us a shiny new edition of *Monopoly*, my brother Mike was finishing Donald Trump's *The Art of the Deal*. I liked *Monopoly* because I could personify a dog moving around the board. Mike liked *Monopoly* because it allowed him to practice everything The Donald taught him about financing, developing, and constructing big ocean-side condominiums on his naïve younger sister and her little dog, too. Mike granted me the less affluent neighborhoods like Baltic or Vermont Avenues and he'd humor me into buying great plots of land with wonderful development potential like New York and Kentucky Avenues. I knew better than to go after Boardwalk and Park Place. Once I even lent him money to finance a hotel on Marvin Gardens, which he conveniently forgot when I landed there.

"That's $2,200," Mike would say.

"I don't have $2,200! I gave $1,500 to you!"

"Donald Trump doesn't care for your excuses. You'll be hearing from the bank."

"Mom!"

Just a few years ago the family tried busting out the old *Monopoly* game on Christmas Eve, but *The Apprentice* was still alive and well inside my brother. He booted mom out of a quaint little house on Oriental Avenue and suckered dad into spending his entire savings on a dilapidated hotel on Pacific Avenue seconds before he landed on Mike's Boardwalk hotel, casino, and arena where his eponymous hockey team played. My parents were so devastated by his behavior that they changed their will to ensure Mike would have nothing to do with their long-term health care or retirement funds.

I can't say that Mike's ultra-competitive nature ruined *Monopoly* and other board games for me (mostly because I'm afraid he'll read this, put me in a headlock, and give me noogies on my head until my overpriced highlights fade out), but every now and again when I'm in my condo, relaxing with a pint of ice cream and a *Felicity* rerun, I can't help but picture Mike jumping from behind the curtains, waving my deed in the air, and demanding I hand over my parking spot and the keys to my storage unit.

Even though games and I aren't exactly peanut butter and chocolate, or even peanut butter and pickles for that matter, I somehow managed to find myself working in the games industry as a promotions coordinator at a company called Wizards of the Coast.

I don't know what I expected when I first started my job, but it wasn't to be waiting at the copy machine behind a guy dressed as a *Star Wars* stormtrooper. At first I thought it was one of those cardboard standees you find at Blockbuster, until he turned around and asked me if I knew how to make double-sided copies. What's more surprising is that I had no one to commiserate with, because no one else thought this was weird. The only questions he got were about the suit's authenticity. (It was the real deal, by the way. Cost a fortune, which may be why he chose to wear it anytime he could.) I work at a place where a dragon is suspended from the lobby ceiling, video game consoles line the conference rooms, and sci-fi villains sit in offices, processing your vacation time and issuing purchase orders. What had I gotten myself into?

It wasn't long before I heard the sounds of trading cards shuffling and dice rolling. I saw the remains of cryptic maps and strange words like *Xen'drik* and *Q'barra* left on whiteboards with the words "DO NOT ERASE. EVER." written over them. I'd walk past meeting rooms and see groups of co-workers gathered around tables or staring intently at what looked like someone giving a presentation, and minutes later they'd be broken up with laughter. No one ever laughed in my meetings. What could these people possibly be talking about?

Finally I worked up the nerve to ask what was going on in there.

"We were playing DUNGEONS & DRAGONS," explained one of my coworkers.

"Like that?" I asked, giving a nod to his polo shirt and khaki pants. I guess I expected him to be wearing some kind of armor, or at least have a sword attached to his expensive snakeskin belt. I didn't know what to expect not only from a DUNGEONS & DRAGONS game, but about the people who played it. Certainly not the normal-looking crowd I saw hunched over the conference room table.

For several years, my relationship with DUNGEONS & DRAGONS (or D&D, as it's commonly known) was neutral. Kind of like the vanilla, no-frills relationship you have with your coworker's spouse because you only see each other once a year at the company holiday party. *Dungeons & Dragons* and I would nod to each other in passing. We said polite good mornings at the coffeepot and smiled at the other's reflection in the mirror when we were both washing our hands at the bathroom sink. D&D didn't bother with me and I didn't bother with it.

Then one day my cubicle neighbor, Teddy, performed a fifty-seven minute monologue about how weaponry in *Dungeons & Dragons* doesn't pay a lot of attention to historical reality.

"You just find things like a falchion being a two-handed scimitar in D&D, and a one-handed infantry sword in history," he explained. "But that's fine. D&D is a game, not a historical simulation."

I politely endured, nodded instinctively, inserted some "wow's" and "oh cools" as needed. And then politeness bit me in the ass.

"If you're interested in historical weaponry, you'd probably love playing," Teddy said. "I'm starting a new group on Monday nights. Why don't you join?"

If niceness were a D&D skill, Teddy would be a trillion-level uber-human. Saying no to Teddy would be like saying no to Winnie the Pooh. Besides, since *Melrose Place* went off the air, Mondays really suck.

I accepted the invitation, then promptly had flashbacks to second grade when a big fat "U" for Unsatisfactory showed up my report card under "cooperation." *Shelly doesn't play well with others. She's a loner, much preferring to lock herself in a bathroom stall and read a book. By the way, she's much too young for Jackie Collins."*

I'd show Mrs. Remy who plays well with others. (And Jackie Collins is a fine role model for an eight-year-old girl, thank you very much.) I suspect *Dungeons & Dragons* groups all over the world are filled with kids who "didn't play well with others." I still wake up in a cold sweat, swatting invisible chunks of playground asphalt from my knees. The words "tag" and "batter up" should only be used in conjunction with the words "sale" and "brownie."

Not wanting to go into the game completely blind, I did a little research. I'm the kind of person who likes to know what I'm getting into before I jump in. I check the weather forecast before I go out, read the cover copy on book jackets before I buy, and stick my toe in a swimming pool before I dive in. If I was going to create a character, how could I not know every facet of the universe she'd be living in? My mother wouldn't even let me ride to the mall with someone's mom without knowing what kind of car she drove, her license number, and who her insurance carrier was. I inherited her cautious nature (in addition to weak ankles, abnormally small ears, and addiction to the Food Network), so in preparation for the game I pored over DUNGEONS & DRAGONS for Dummies, the Player's Handbook, and the Monster Manual.

Contrary to what I believed, the Player's Handbook has nothing to do with why men don't return your call for three days and refuse to spend more than forty dollars on a first date. It's the player's guidebook to maneuvering throughout the D&D universe. I brought the Monster Manual to Starbucks and enjoyed a tall non-fat sugar-free vanilla latte while reading about the two hundred-plus monsters waiting in the dark to pounce on my soon-to-be alter ego and her friends. Insurance policy be damned! Does State Farm offer protection from flesh golems?

DUNGEONS & DRAGONS for Dummies got me through fifty minutes on the treadmill every Monday, Wednesday, and Friday. (It also got me a couple of charley horses and quads that look like two watermelons when stuffed into skinny jeans, but that's a different story.) When a fellow gym rat noted my reading material he raised his eyebrows and said, "Well, that's one way to ensure people leave you alone."

Forgetting for a moment that I am not Astrid Bellagio, 134-year-old elf sorceress (and I cannot blink this boy into a nasty bout with athlete's foot), I gave him the stink eye and said, "Don't knock it until you've tried it."

"Oh, I've tried it," he said. "Back in 1982 when I was twelve years old with chronic acne and a Mountain Dew addiction. It was rockin'."

Oh, right. The stereotypes. I knew all about them—I believed them, too. Basements, incense, black cloaks, and Doritos-stained fingers attached to the limbs of unstable, social outcasts. Nerds, geeks, dweebs, dorks. Kids who got stuffed headfirst into the high school cafeteria trash cans across the country. (D&D is played worldwide, but I can't picture a Finnish kid stuffing someone in a garbage can due to some warped romantic view of Scandinavians. Besides, there's no drinking age and it's dark all the time there. How can they all not get along?)

Kids who were into D&D were sent to the principal's office because their teachers caught them doodling dragons and elf mistresses in the margins of their history notes. Never mind the great detailing of their dragons. It's a dragon, for goodness' sake! That which we don't understand belongs in detention.

And it was always boys, right? Girls never played. We girls were too busy counting our jelly bracelets and daydreaming about going to drive-in movies with the cast from *The Outsiders* to play games. Now, if Ponyboy and Johnny went on the lam because Johnny killed an umber hulk instead of a rival gang member, I for one would have traded in my *Sweet Valley High* books for the *Dungeon Master's Guide*. But alas, my one hundred and thirty-seven black jelly bracelets had much better things to do than play a silly old game. And up until a few months ago, my one hundred and thirty-seven pairs of black shoes and I were much too busy to play a silly old game.

A girlfriend once defined board games as "games that make you bored." I've also heard "tedious," "time-consuming," "not my chosen way to relax," "complicated," "childish," and "for boys," all from women, all in regard to games.

Complicated? Some. Time-consuming? If you're lucky. Boring? Not this game. And it doesn't even require a board. As much as I tried to fight it (and I did try to fight it), D&D won me over like the quiet, outcast wallflower that is so not your type but is kind of funny and has great manners. What's one date, you think? It never hurts to have another friend, right? Next thing you know, you're going steady and can't wait for your friends to meet D&D.

The Geek Factor

Let's start at the beginning. Thirty-some years ago, *DUNGEONS & DRAGONS* first hit the scene and gave kids a reason other than tornado scares and Ms. Pacman to hang out in their basements. We've all seen the pictures, heard the anecdotes, and watched the funny videos on VH1's *I Love the 70's* of scrawny, post-pubescent boys with shrunken rugby-shirts and car wash bangs hanging over their pimply foreheads. Nerds, right? Oh, come on! It was 1975! Everyone looked like that. Even Leif Garret had a pimple now and then, and who didn't wear their t-shirts and Toughskins a little past their prime?

I remember a kid in my seventh grade homeroom we'll call "Greg." No, wait—that was his name. Let's call him Chachi.

Chachi wore the same black trenchcoat and black Dickies every day. His dark hair had so much dandruff, he looked like his head was encased in its own personal snow globe. We were terrified of Chachi and his beady-eyed stare—the way he'd glare at us as we walked past his desk to the chalkboard to conjugate a verb. The creepy tunes he'd hum instead of answering Mr. Fletcher's questions regarding Joan of Arc. He wasn't smart enough to be a nerd, so we dubbed him a psycho. We *knew* he played D&D. He *worshiped* D&D. He's probably playing D&D right now, we'd marvel, watching him tear apart his bologna sandwich in the cafeteria like it was a skeletal beast.

We didn't know one lick about D&D. Like how you need friends to play, or how D&D helps foster social skills, builds confidence, and gives players a sense of community. How Chachi's roleplaying group provided an outlet for his imagination. How his creativity flourished outside the margins of his notebooks. How if he applied himself he'd have kicked our butts in math and won creative writing competitions. Chachi had friends—somewhere—a group of friends he still hangs out with today. I know this because our hometown newspaper just did a story on him. He's a pretty big deal over at some Fortune 500 company. Even with job pressures and a new set of twins, Chachi

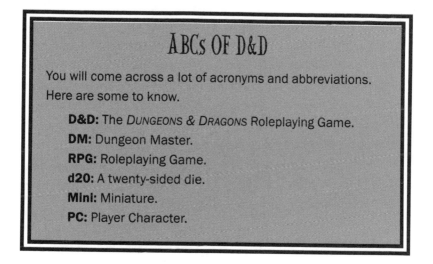

ABCs OF D&D

You will come across a lot of acronyms and abbreviations. Here are some to know.

D&D: The DUNGEONS & DRAGONS Roleplaying Game.

DM: Dungeon Master.

RPG: Roleplaying Game.

d20: A twenty-sided die.

Mini: Miniature.

PC: Player Character.

still finds time to get together with his friends for a little rolling of the dice now and again. He says his background in zombie hunting has helped prepare him for a few of his boardroom encounters.

Still, the stereotypes are harder to remove than grass stains on your favorite jeans. (By the way, why were you sliding around in the grass in your favorite jeans anyway?)

I have a good group of girlfriends. I'm lucky, I know. As you might expect, none of them has ever played DUNGEONS & DRAGONS or even been in the same room with people who were playing. It's hard for me to imagine D&D as a blank slate, having been in contact with it in some vague form all of these years. You can't walk to the copier at Wizards of the Coast without hearing the sound of dice hitting Formica. Still, I was surprised that these women didn't even know the game involved dice. I decided to conduct my own informal focus group.

The guinea pigs (and yes, I just called my friends pigs, even after all they've done for me) include five women. Subject A is a mother of a toddler. Her most prized possessions are her gym membership and her TiVo. Subject B is also the mother of a toddler. She makes her own Christmas cards, loves animals, and couldn't name four television shows currently in prime time rotation if her baby's acceptance into a Montessori school depended on it. Subjects C, D, and E are unmarried but in various stages of long-term relationships. One owns a record label and is cooler than all the cool people I know put together. The other two are subscribers to *People* and *Lucky* and regularly drop the equivalent of my mortgage payment on designer handbags, only to go back a week later and drop my car payment on the matching wallet. All of these women are social, smart, and enjoy spending time together. I emailed them each a list of questions asking for their honest perception of my newfound hobby.

Question 1: What do you know about DUNGEONS & DRAGONS?

Subject A: It's complicated and geared toward boys who
   collect comic books and make sounds when they talk
   for more emphasis. ("We took the speed boat out today.
   Vrrrrrrrroooooooommmmm. Totally huge waves pummeled us!
   Smaaaack, smaaaack, smaaaaack!")

Subject B: It's some kind of complicated game that the weird nerdy
   brother of a friend of mine played. I have no idea what kind of
   game, but I know there is a book involved because Ken (the
   brother) was ALWAYS carrying it around with him.

Subject C: It's a fantasy board game that mostly super-smart nerdy
   types play because there are thousands of rules you have to
   learn. I think it involves unicorns, which might be kind of cool
   in a thirteen-year-old girl sort of way.

Subject D: Is that thing still around? The dragons are Satan and the
   dungeon is hell. It's a euphemism for everything that is evil in
   the world. Actually I just made that up to piss you off. You still
   work for the company, right?

OUT OF THE DUNGEON

People still play DUNGEONS & DRAGONS? I hear that a lot. The answer is yes, and you might be surprised by just who has either copped to playing or is rumored to play. **Vin Diesel** is out of the dungeon. He even wrote the foreword to the book, *Thirty Years of Adventure: A Celebration of DUNGEONS & DRAGONS*. He may not be saying it, but they sure did play it. Who's in with Vin?

* **Stephen Colbert,** insanely funny writer, actor, and host of *The Colbert Report*. Out since 1976.
* **Hal Sparks,** musician and comedian who had a starring role on *Queer as Folk*.
* **Ben Kweller,** musician. Out since around eight years old.
* **Wil Wheaton,** actor, writer, and one of my first crushes. Out since 1979.
* **Sherman Alexie,** poet, novelist, screenwriter, and literary force not to be reckoned with. Out since around eight years old.
* **Mark Tremonti,** member of the band Alter Bridge. Out since around eight years old.
* **James Merendino,** writer and director of Sundance Film Festival favorite *SLC Punk* as well as *Magicians, Terrified,* and *Trespassing.*
* **John Rogers,** creator of the hit WB Kids show *Jackie Chan Adventures* and writer of over ten feature films.
* **John Frank Rosenblum,** writer and producer who has worked on such films as *Dr. Who, Trailer Park, Mimic,* and *Imposter.*
* **Laurell K. Hamilton,** *New York Times* best-selling author of the *Anita Blake, Vampire Hunter* series. Out since junior year of high school.
* **Sharyn McCrumb,** *New York Times* best-selling author. Out since the early 80's.
* **Dave Meyers,** music video and commercial director.
* **Ed Robertson,** founding member of the rock group Barenaked Ladies. Out since fifth grade.
* **David X. Cohen,** Emmy Award-winning producer and writer of the series *Futurama*. Out since middle school.
* **Genndy Tartakovsky,** creator of the television series *Star Wars: Clone Wars*. Out since the early 80's.
* **Matthew Rhodes,** producer of films such as *Auggie Rose, An Unfinished Life,* and *September Tapes*. Out since fifteen years old.
* **Tom DeSanto,** writer and producer who has worked on such films as *X2, X-Men United, Apt Pupil,* and the live-action *Transformers* film. Out since eighth grade.

Not such shabby company to be keeping, right? Come on, people. We know there are more of you out there. If your fellow superstars can confess to phone sex with psychics and more lifts and tucks than a hotel mattress, you can admit to a little dabbling in the dungeon.

Subject E: It's some kind of "role-play" game with a stigma attached because people must act like trolls and wizards and talk in funny voices.

Question 2: What stereotypes do you have about the game?

Subject A: I think D&D is a game for pre-pubescent boys who meet up with all of their friends that play in a basement and form a secret club they name something like "The Dragon Slayers." They have secret handshakes and meet up in secret places and one of them may have a secret passageway in their home where they meet. They make moms nervous because they are so secretive.

Subject B: It's sort of creepy that guys (never girls) would sit around a table and "act out" a game.

Subject C: Mostly just nerds play it.

Subject D: You have to dress up in weird costumes, talk in weird accents, and spend days in your basements pretending to be wizards and knights so you can someday cast spells on people who cut you off in traffic or keep you on hold for too long.

Subject E: As far as I know . . . the people that play this game hang out in their basements all the time, all consumed by this game, dressing up as their characters and carrying on as though they were actually in the game. I guess I would classify them as gamer geeks.

Question 3: Do you know anyone who plays?

All five subjects answered with a resounding, "No."

No? Really? Hmm, maybe I forgot to mention my new hobby.

Can't say their answers were too surprising. They've all come to the same conclusion that D&D is "hard" and you need to have a basement, bad skin, and a secret handshake to learn it. I have none of those things (at least not right now. The skin thing is subject to change at any moment), but clearly I have my work cut out for me. Although it's a small control group, it's probably a very accurate sampling. (Minus Subject D's responses. Her existence is based solely on the ability to make me angry, like calling in the pre-TiVo days during the first ten minutes of *Melrose Place* without fail just to ask, "What are you doing?" She knows what I was doing!)

Here's the deal. I don't expect you to change your mind about who was playing the game in 1982 and who, if anyone, you think is playing the game now. If we can't change the stereotypes, we might as well embrace them. Is it weird to foster a strong social network, or to allow a game to create a bond between people? Maybe for some, sure. As adults, friendships become more ephemeral and downtime a rare commodity, so finding time to get together with your friends week after week to "play a game" says a lot. If a nerd is someone who is hyper-smart, a tad socially retarded, creative, strategic, and does math problems and crossword puzzles as a form of relaxation, then yes, you're right. Nerds probably do play D&D. Even though I haven't let "X" equal anything other than bad judgment and beer goggles since freshman year of college (okay, maybe junior year. Or last summer. Whatever), I'd be honored to be counted among the nerds. Nerds are in. Everyone's embracing the nerd these days. My very mainstream and fashion forward friend just showed up to happy hour with a beaded clutch proclaiming "I LOVE NERDS."

"You do not," I argued. "You like overgrown frat boys who still have roommates and posters advertising beer as breakfast food."

"Nuh uh," she argued back. "Nerds rock."

See what I mean? The geek shall inherit the Earth, indeed. We're adopting nerd culture faster than Angelina Jolie adopts orphaned villages. But apparently nerd culture is a la carte.

You Might Be a Roleplayer If...

So this roleplaying thing . . . it conjures up all sort of images, doesn't it? Couples therapy. *(Mr. Johnson, try to take on the persona of the toilet seat and really dig into how it feels to be left up all the time.)* Or that kinky, middle-aged couple from downstairs. *(Mrs. Salamedia! I had no idea you were a cheerleader! You've got to be the most flexible member of the AARP!)*

What the heck is roleplaying? You could always look it up in the dictionary:

A psychotherapeutic technique, designed to reduce the conflict inherent in various social situations, in which participants act out particular behavioral roles in order to expand their awareness of differing points of view.

Still bringing up those awful images of your neighbors, huh? Let's check in with the informal focus group for a less formal definition.

Subject A: Role-playing: (rol-*playin') To play a role. Pretend. Step in and act like someone else. "Frontin'."

Subject B: Kinky, yet well thought out sex. Who has time for that?

Subject C: I hardly know anything about roleplaying but when I'm forced to think of what it might entail, I think of a group of people sitting around pretending to be other people. Possibly they're even dressed up in character. It's kind of frightening, if you ask me.

Subject D: Pretending to be someone you aren't, usually in regard to sex. Why do you ask? Are you seeing someone?

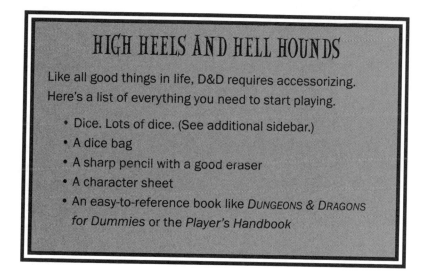

HIGH HEELS AND HELL HOUNDS

Like all good things in life, D&D requires accessorizing.
Here's a list of everything you need to start playing.

- Dice. Lots of dice. (See additional sidebar.)
- A dice bag
- A sharp pencil with a good eraser
- A character sheet
- An easy-to-reference book like DUNGEONS & DRAGONS for Dummies or the Player's Handbook

Subject E: Roleplaying makes me think of two things. One: A naughty couple who dresses up and acts out various roles (such as cop and robber, nurse and doctor, etc.) and then they have kinky sex. And two: Every Sunday this group gets together at the community center near my house. They get dressed like knights in heavy armor and have real sword fights.

Well, okay. This is probably why a female D&D player told me to be careful when referring to myself as a roleplayer. Apparently you'll be branding yourself a dominant nurse who's handy with a billy club.

Let's flash back to high school. I know, I know, even worse images but bear with me. Did you have a debate club? They ran those mock trials after school? Sometimes they competed with other schools that thought this was a more productive way to spend after-school hours than trying to beat your brother's high score in Frogger. *Charles is the plastic bottle factory and Susan's Greenpeace. Susan wants to shut Charles down. Charles thinks plastic is fantastic.*

No bells ringing? Okay, let's go back a few more years. Remember your pal Barbie? You spent hours brushing her hair and then eventually chopped it off, only to cry over it because your big brother lied—it didn't grow back. What is Barbie if not a giant mini with synthetic hair?

You and Butch Cut Barbie furnished her dream house, cruised in her pink corvette, and walked her dog Beauty, the ginormous white Collie with a faulty equilibrium. Your friends came over with their Barbies and you orchestrated pool parties and swapped clothes and your plastic people went on double dates while cruising around in their pink corvettes. Eventually Barbie lost her charm and my mom stopped buying dolls when she found them taped to my brother's Hot Wheels tracks.

What I lacked in respect for dolls I made up for with stuffed animals. I had bears, bunnies, seals, dogs, ducks, and frogs. They had names, backstories, husbands and wives, children, and jobs. Froggy O'Hara owned a pillow factory. He married Green Rabbito, an opera singer. She still sings Christmas carols to my mother every year. They lived happily in their makeshift city, driving around in their shoebox car until Froggy sold his pillow empire and bought the Atlanta Braves. He left Greenie penniless and took up with Butch Cut Barbie and her pink Corvette. Greenie was devastated until she took up with Tubby Pistelle, a crooked cop, who never admitted having any part in the breaking of Butch Cut Barbie's hyper-extended legs. My stuffed animals had more storylines than sweeps week on daytime television.

Okay, maybe Mom was right and I should have been playing outdoors with a kickball and a Big Wheel instead of chillin' in the basement, acting as mayor of my own private Animal Planet. And maybe I just disclosed too much information. That's not the point. The point is, women have been roleplaying their whole lives.

Women love conversation and get-togethers and pretending to be something we're not. Oh, just admit it. I confessed I had adulterous stuffed animals. You can confess to telling a few white lies. *Would You Rather . . .* , *I Went on Vacation and Brought . . .* , *I Never . . .* , *Truth or Dare*—all games.

House, doctor, tea party—all roleplaying. *DUNGEONS & DRAGONS*—*a roleplaying game*. It was made for women. Why hasn't anyone told us yet?

Still don't believe me? That's okay. I was expecting some resistance. Think about heroes for a moment. D&D's most popular female characters all have a few things in common: They're buxom, built, and badass. If you and your girlfriends saw Lidda, a halfling rogue from the *DUNGEONS & DRAGONS* universe, walk up to Panda Express in the mall food court, no doubt you'd raise an eyebrow and give her leather-and-armor jumpsuit a very dramatic once-over. The conversation to follow would go something like this:

"Hey, check out the shoulder pads. Is that Milli or Vanilli?"

"I hope the woolly mammoth she rode on isn't blocking us in."

"Yikes! Does she not have a mirror?"

"Or a friend?"

This of course would lead to pinky swears and promises that you would never let your friends leave the house with food in their teeth, toilet paper on their shoe, or a giant wedgie careening up their buttocks.

Maybe that's a bit extreme. I mean, how many of us actually eat in mall food courts? If the fashion-challenged Lidda crossed your path, you'd probably be thinking at least one of the above. But riddle me this: If Lara Croft's *Tomb Raider* threads happened to get mixed up in your dry cleaning, before you called the cleaner to complain, would you maybe try them on? Just once? Sure you would. You'd be cleaning out the refrigerator and paying your mortgage or jogging on your mini trampoline watching a *What Not to Wear* marathon while wearing them. You couldn't pass a mirror without looking yourself up and down, maybe see how the outfit moves when you throw a few shadow punches. Look how it holds in that perpetual stomach bulge that gives the illusion you just finished nineteen pounds of baked beans and a case of beer. Your quads suddenly resemble two boa constrictors that just feasted on an orchard of cantaloupes. And are those biceps under there? Hubba bubba! A *hiiii-ya!* would undoubtedly escape your lips and you'd kick your leg higher than the hemline on a teenager's skirt. Not

Gaming Session

only would you look good wearing it, you would feel darn good too. Why? Because women want female heroes. We like kicking the bad guy's ass. Wonder Woman, Xena, Buffy, Sydney from *Alias*: Even if she is married to Ben Affleck, Jennifer Garner's alter ego had it going on. And who wouldn't love an invisible jet and a truth-provoking magic lasso? Come to think of it, Wonder Woman's red boots are pretty bitchin' too.

In a D&D game, players are typically part of a team (or a "party" of adventurers) united in the effort to achieve a common goal. What makes roleplaying games (or RPGs) different from other games is that generally there are no winners or losers. Now that's my kind of game.

Understandably, you might want a visual. Close your eyes and picture this. Ah, never mind. Open them so you can read this. It's like this: a group of people sits around a table, similar to how they would sit if they were scrapbooking or eating Chinese food or planning the neighborhood's next block party. There are usually food and drinks scattered about and most likely some kind of grid or map in the center of the table, with various miniatures (or minis) taking their places on it. The Dungeon Master (DM) is probably at the head of the table. He will have a screen set up in front of him. This is where the DM weaves the tale, which includes various entry points where the player characters must decide on an action. After a lot of dice rolling, an order is determined and players take turns controlling the fate of their characters. Taking turns, or a series of "rounds," continues until victory or defeat has been accomplished. Then the story continues. It's essentially cooperative storytelling around the table—something everyone has done and enjoyed. It's not charades. It's not an audition. You will not be judged on how funny or smart or British you can sound. In fact, your butt seldom leaves the chair cushion with the exception of bathroom breaks or refilling the guacamole. It's quite relaxing, really—with the added excitement of all the imagined spellcasting and sword swinging.

Still wary about going fist to claw with a red dragon? Don't write it off until you've considered the following statements:

1. You like listening to and telling stories.
2. You like storytelling games in which you work *with* your fellow players, not *against* them.
3. You like smack downs, beat downs, and low downs, but a trip downtown curbs your enthusiasm against venting your rage.
4. You like adventure.
5. You like your friends.
6. You don't like your friends and would like to make new ones.

If you agree with at least one of the above, dig out your dice and sharpen your pencils. You might be a dragon lady after all. DUNGEONS & DRAGONS satisfies the requirements for all five statements above (number six is a maybe—no promises) but perhaps the most unique game-play element is that it's noncompetitive. Hear that? Noncompetitive, as in it takes the group working together to overcome an obstacle. You take turns, advise and protect one another, even heal or be healed when the going gets too tough. I know! That's not a game—that's friendship!

Dungeons 'n Dragons Rulz!

Yes, the rumors are true. DUNGEONS & DRAGONS has rules. Lots of them. You'll learn some of them here and some will start to make sense while you're playing. The rest of the rules? (Dungeon Masters need to cover their eyes now.) Don't worry about them. The beauty of this game is you don't have to know how to play to start playing. How many times has a friend taught you how to hem your jeans with double-sided tape or use liquid eyeliner without looking like you're hankering for a bite out of someone's neck? One thing I've learned about gamers is that they love sharing knowledge about their favorite pastime. Remember the level fifty-four gnome warrior? Some of our most impassioned conversations were about the advantages of leveling up a carefully crafted character in the *World of Warcraft* computer game.

Him: You need eighty gold pieces for a +60% mount. Of course you'll get a discount if you have an honorable reputation in Stormwind.

Me: You mean I can have a pony?

Him: It's not a pony, it's a mount. And you need to be level forty before you can even consider it. You're still at level one.

Me: Can I get a parakeet?

D&D fans aren't much different. The group you're adventuring with will show you what to do. All you have to do is ask. By the way, you can have your pony in the D&D universe, even at 1st level . . . as long as you have the gold pieces.

One important rule you'll want to learn right away is that gender doesn't matter. A woman can play a male character and a man can play a woman.

My character would kick ass just as much if she were a man. My group's number one fighter is a 3'2" dwarf named Ursula who is brought to life by a real-world 5'1" new mother named Lucy. I highly doubt Lucy plows through Babies 'R Us brandishing her greatsword, demanding to know where the natural embroidered burp clothes are. That's what's great about DUNGEONS & DRAGONS. It affords the player an opportunity to be someone else in a safe environment, as opposed to outside the bus station or on a first date.

But the number-one rule and for some the hardest to learn is this: Have fun. As our friends on Sesame Street taught us, it's all about cooperation—not competition. Now if only we could take that from the play mat to the playground.

Die-Curious Female Seeks Friends for Adventuring and Hellraising

So now you think you might be ready to give the old twenty-sided die a try? Curious about what really goes on in a game of D&D? Wondering what the heck a twenty-sided die looks like? Let me enlighten you.

You will show up for your first game and be welcomed by someone's mom—probably the Dungeon Master's. She'll point you in the general direction of the basement and ask if you wouldn't mind bringing down another case of orange soda and four more bags of chips. You notice with some sadness that none of the chips are of the baked variety and wish you'd had the foresight to bring your own snacks. In the basement you'll find your way to the round table by the glowing embers of candlelight. You'll be asked to adorn a black cloak, prick your left index finger, and repeat the code you spent days memorizing and—oh, come on! Do I even need to tell you I'm kidding?

· ·

The reality of what to expect goes something like this: You'll meet your friends pretty much anywhere there is a table and chairs. You can bring snacks to share and yes, in some cases it will be Cheetos and full-sugar soda. For my first game, I showed up with a Ziploc bag full of Kashi cereal and snap peas and was promptly berated.

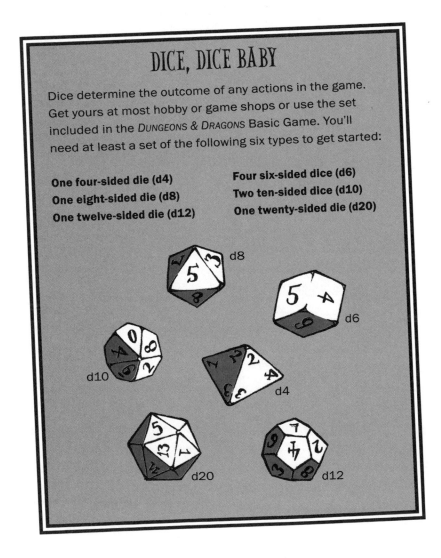

DICE, DICE BABY

Dice determine the outcome of any actions in the game. Get yours at most hobby or game shops or use the set included in the DUNGEONS & DRAGONS Basic Game. You'll need at least a set of the following six types to get started:

One four-sided die (d4)
One eight-sided die (d8)
One twelve-sided die (d12)

Four six-sided dice (d6)
Two ten-sided dice (d10)
One twenty-sided die (d20)

Know what's better than a catnip—filled, remote—control—activated mouse toy? A set of fancy new dice! Cats love rolling dice almost as much as a bunch of drunken bachelors at a craps table in Vegas. If you don't want to find d2Os in your sling—backs or spend long nights monitoring a kitty with digestive issues, keep your dice out of kitty's range. Oh, yeah—same goes for kids.

"What character are you playing?" one fellow adventurer asked. "A rabbit?"

"You are the antithesis of a D&D player," another claimed. "Couldn't you at least have brought Frosted Flakes?"

Essential to the game are players (at least two), someone willing to be a Dungeon Master, and an adventure that the Dungeon Master has prepared. It's also helpful to have the *Player's Handbook*, your own set of dice (sharing is caring but borrowing your neighbor's dice every three minutes gets really annoying), character sheets (more on these later), a miniature, a map (for those visual types), sharpened pencils, erasers, and if you're really number-phobic, a calculator. Sounds like you're about to take the SATs, right? Having done both, I assure you, D&D is a whole lot more fun.

My group consists of seven players, including the Dungeon Master. We're all professional thirty-somethings ranging from Brand Managers to a Media Planner to a Vice President. Half of the players in my group are the proud parents of five real-life human minis while the rest are parents to four dogs and five cats. We eat vegetables, pay our bills, have health insurance, and celebrate holidays. Pretty normal people so far.

Amok and Jak

In addition to Lucy the warrior mommy, the group includes Armando, a self-proclaimed dork who plays Jak, a changeling rogue. Hank is a funny and laid-back father of three who plays a half-elf ranger named Yakama. Calvin, a charming egomaniac who loves himself more than Joan Rivers loves dissing celebrities, plays the human cleric Amok. Helena, a brainiac with a newly acquired MBA, plays the shifter monk Tenoctris. Teddy, our Dungeon Master, really is a Dungeon Master as far as I can tell.

PARTY LIKE IT'S 1982

A good D&D party doesn't need a DJ and plastic monkey charms hanging from your drinks. You need a well-rounded group of adventurers played by people you can stand knocking dice with for a good two hours (at least). Here's getting to know my party people:

Real Name	Character Name	Character Role
Lucy	Ursula	Dwarf fighter
Hank	Yakama	Half-elf ranger
Calvin	Amok	Human cleric
Armando	Jak	Changeling rogue
Helena	Tenoctris	Shifter monk
Shelly	Astrid	Elf sorcerer
Teddy	—	Dungeon Master

While Teddy draws the map, setting the stage for our adventure, we set our miniatures on the playing field. The mini (because D&D is all about abbreviations, as you'll soon find out) represents your character on the playing field. Each player, as well as the various beasts you'll encounter, will have one. I remember the day Teddy handed me my Astrid.

"Will this work for your sorcerer?" he asked, tossing the tiny plastic figure onto my desk. "I might have some others in my car."

In his car? I wonder if he uses them to qualify for the carpool lane.

Your mini will probably find its way to you via a more traditional route, like from a store. There are over six hundred miniatures available and all come fully painted, which is good if you don't have a steady hand or the patience to decorate your own thirty-millimeter figure. If you're the kind of person who needs to change clothes more times a day than a newborn who recently discovered strained carrots, you could look into painting your own.

Seeing our band of plastic people scattered about in various corners on the play mat reminds me of the first day of school. I wonder if any of them are hoping someone braver than they are comes over to talk to them. I wonder if they want to go home. I feel a tug in my gut from wanting to rescue Astrid, to make her a brown bag lunch of liverwurst sandwiches and blueberry yogurt and comb her plastic yellow hair. But, I remind myself,

Ursula and Yakama

if Astrid's going to be a successful sorceress someday she needs her independence. She looks small and brave on the play mat. Her purple cloak is set in a windblown position, baring the tops of her sculpted thighs. She's brandishing a magical staff over her head like it's a foam finger at a sporting match. *I'm number one!,* she claims. Maybe she's confident. Or maybe she's delusional.

"Astrid looks like a stripper," Calvin says. His character is a cleric and a comment like that is a tad inappropriate for a holy person.

"Whatever she looks like," I say, "she ain't looking at you. She thinks Amok is a sissy. And he has bad breath."

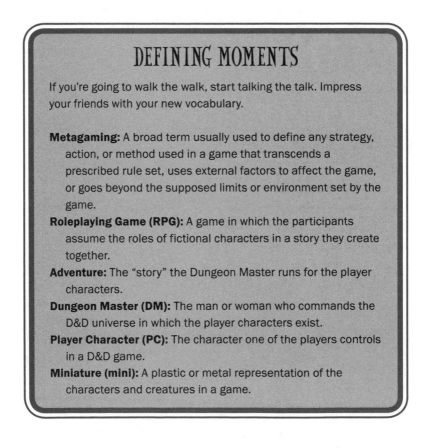

DEFINING MOMENTS

If you're going to walk the walk, start talking the talk. Impress your friends with your new vocabulary.

Metagaming: A broad term usually used to define any strategy, action, or method used in a game that transcends a prescribed rule set, uses external factors to affect the game, or goes beyond the supposed limits or environment set by the game.

Roleplaying Game (RPG): A game in which the participants assume the roles of fictional characters in a story they create together.

Adventure: The "story" the Dungeon Master runs for the player characters.

Dungeon Master (DM): The man or woman who commands the D&D universe in which the player characters exist.

Player Character (PC): The character one of the players controls in a D&D game.

Miniature (mini): A plastic or metal representation of the characters and creatures in a game.

Astrid and Amok

"You guys are *metagaming*," Helena, the big old smarty pants, says. Metagaming is a no-no meaning projecting my (the player) everyday knowledge on to my character (Astrid).

"Apparently Helena thinks you're a foul-breathed sissy in real life," I explain to Calvin in case that one sailed by his immaculately groomed head. "Too bad you don't know an *induce altoids* spell."

"Well, when Astrid is fighting for her last breath on the side of a dirt road somewhere," Calvin says, "Amok might be too busy with a fluoride treatment to heal her."

Ouch.

Dear Diary,

I met some new friends today. I was running some errands at Fashion Valley Mall when my sugar level dropped to an all-time low and I needed sustenance immediately. Chocolate peanut butter caramel cheesecake or bust. Of course there was a line to get seated and being a party of one, there was no way they'd seat me in the dining room. I opted for the bar instead and I'm glad I did! There was this cute little dwarf named Ursula causing all sorts of mayhem at the end of the bar. I think she was hustling patrons by playing rock, paper, scissors or something. Anyway, after I finished my cheesecake, I joined the spectators watching her mastery. For a dwarf she's really dexterous. Quite the crowd had gathered, and before long I felt something slimy along my backside. The creep cleric next to me had this innocent expression on his face so I immediately knew he was guilty. I gave him an elbow to the gut.

"What?" he asked, mock shock oozing out his pores (or was that his cologne?). "It was my spiritual weapon!"

"Spiritual weapons don't cast themselves," I said, ready to kick the perv in the shins.

Prospective battle caught the dwarf's attention and she was by my side pronto. She shoved a gnarled little fist under his chin and told him if he came near me again, she'd take her greatsword to his spiritual weapon. Yeah. That spiritual weapon.

Lucky for him, his friend Yakama intervened and apologized for his friend's wander-lusting digits. He even bought us drinks as a peace offering. Ursula can knock them back! My tolerance needs a little work.

Before long we heard a crash in the kitchen. Ursula was on her feet, once again showing that surprising dexterity. Apparently a shape-shifting rogue found his way onto the line and thought it would be funny if he shifted his shape into a cockroach. Ursula knew him from a poker game she used to play in and she introduced us to Jak. Amok ordered a round of shots that felt like the breath of a hell hound going down. Three hours into our impromptu happy hour, a slight (and hairy!) brunette monk approached our table and whispered something to Yakama.

"This is Tenoctris," he said. "And she could use our help with something."

"If you're feeling up to it," she added. Was she looking at me? I think she was looking at me!

The girl could really use a makeover and I could sure help with that but there was a much bigger adventure in store. The makeover would probably be more of a challenge but hey, I'm up for anything.

Love, Astrid

DEFINING MOMENTS

Alignment: Your character's stance in the battle between good and evil.

Battle Grid: A great visual for those who need spatial assistance. The battle grid (or play mat) is a 1-inch grid used to show where the action is taking place.

Class: Your character's chosen career. There are eleven classes described in the *Player's Handbook*: barbarian, bard, cleric, druid, fighter, monk, paladin, ranger, rogue, sorcerer, and wizard.

Experience Points (XP): The measure of your character's success. Experience points are earned after you and your party overcome challenges such as recovering a long-lost map or defeating an angry band of trolls.

Level: The measure or your character's advancement or the power of spells. Your level is comparable to the grade you are in school (if school went up to twentieth grade and beyond).

Mini: Short for miniature. Your mini represents you on the battle grid.

Race: Your character's species. The common races include humans, dwarves, elves, gnomes, half-elves, half-orcs, and halflings.

Boots of Levitation! No more trying to see the band from behind a perm gone awry. Rise to any occasion!

Chapter Two

BUILDING CHARACTER

Lots of D&D players will tell you that building your character is one of the best parts of the game. Not since I spent an entire day at an outlet mall have I been required to do so much math, but the payoff is worth it. Sure, you can play DUNGEONS & DRAGONS out of the box using the ready-made characters from the Basic Game. But call me selfish; I chose to build my own. Would she

GET A LIFE

No need to panic if the guy in the cubicle next to you isn't a part-time Dungeon Master. Creating a character is one the most fun parts of the game. There are loads of references to help you out. Check out the following:

> DUNGEONS & DRAGONS for Dummies
> The Player's Handbook
> www.wizards.com/dnd
> www.playdnd.com

Of course, it doesn't hurt to have a Dungeon Master sitting next to you.

look like me? Share my sense of humor? Have the same weak ankles passed down from her grandmother?

As it turns out, building character takes as long in the D&D world as it does in real life. At least all I needed this time was a pencil and paper instead of a sweaty summer working at Pizza Hut.

One of the coolest things about D&D is gender equality. As in real life, whichever gender you choose to play is a matter of personal preference but unlike the real world, female and male characters are equals. Sorry, ladies, there are no bonus points for being able to walk in heels over cobblestones or remembering the anniversary of the day your best friend's divorce was final. There are also no deductions for clumpy mascara or visible panty lines. Come to think of it, maybe there should be.

Prior to my first game, I spent some serious quality time with Teddy creating my character. By "creating my character," I mean using my mechanical pencil to twist my hair into an updo and building Stonehenge-like creations with twenty-sided dice, while Teddy filled out my character sheet. Admittedly, I also got a "U" in listening skills.

When I was seven years old I told my schoolmate, Christopher Adams, that I was magic and could make his most desired wish come true. He wished for a puppy. I shut my eyes, furrowed my brow, concentrated all my might, and granted his wish. The next day, he told me he awoke next to a yellow furball and a faceful of puppy breath. I feigned nonchalance at my magical prowess, but really, I was amazed at my own abilities and pissed off I couldn't make a puppy appear on my own pillow. Even years later, it seemed only natural that I would choose to play a sorcerer. Good thing the group I was joining was short one *magic missile* thrower.

First things first. To get started you'll need a D&D character sheet to record all of your character's statistics and vital information. You can find these in the back of the *Player's Handbook* or download them from the website **www.wizards.com/dnd**, or if you're really adventurous you can build your own (see Chapter Six). The character sheet is essential. You'll reference this more than a pocket mirror after a spinach salad. It's like a driver's license on steroids because not only does it include your height, weight and gender, but also Intelligence, Constitution, Strength, special abilities, gear, bank account, and much more. If only we were forced to carry character sheets in real life. You'd know before you wasted make-up on a first date if the guy you're ogling across the way has what it takes to charm your parents or if he's intelligent, affluent, and as dull as the corner on a kid-proof coffee table.

But She Has a Pretty Face

It's time to dip into the DUNGEONS & DRAGONS gene pool. All that Mr. Rogers tutelage is true: Every character is special. Your character has outstanding abilities sometimes based on race or class and some that were the result of some high die rolling on your part. No matter what, your character stands out. Remember the kid in school who wasn't a good reader but was always picked first for kickball? Or maybe you're a lousy cook but no one can write

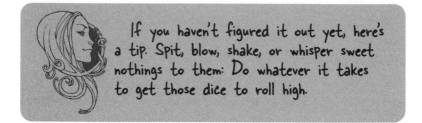

If you haven't figured it out yet, here's a tip. Spit, blow, shake, or whisper sweet nothings to them: Do whatever it takes to get those dice to roll high.

a cursive 'J' like you. I have a memory like a sieve, but I'm an oddly talented rhymer and I'm pretty good at accessorizing. Unfortunately, there are no bonus points for knowing which necklace to wear with a scoop neck. (The answer would be none, by the way. Your décolletage is your best accessory. Try some drop earrings instead.)

It's the same for your D&D characters. Arguably, the most important numbers on the character sheet are your character's *ability scores*. These numbers define a character's score in six key abilities.

Strength (Str): The ability that measures a character's physical power. Important for fighters, rangers, paladins, barbarians, monks, and any character who intends to hit things a lot.

Dexterity (Dex): The ability that measures a character's coordination, reflexes, nimbleness, and balance. Important for rogues, anyone wearing light or no armor (like sorcerers), and archer-types.

Constitution (Con): The ability that measures a character's physical health and endurance. Important for everyone, especially the warrior types who get hit a lot.

Intelligence (Int): The ability that measures a character's learning and reasoning skills. Important for wizards and other smarty-pants classes.

Wisdom (Wis): The ability that measure's a character's will power, common sense, and intuition. Important for clerics, druids, and other characters with a spiritual side.

Charisma (Cha): The ability that measures a character's personality, charm, leadership skills, and physical attractiveness. Important for sorcerers, bards, and those who prefer to talk their way out of a fight.

Depending on your character, you'll assign scores to each of these categories or, much like real life, leave it up to fate. Fate in this case is the bag of dice jingling in your pocket. Abilities generally range between 3 and 18; average score is a 10 or 11. Sorcerers are charming creatures so they'll have higher scores in Charisma, as opposed to fighters who will obviously be above average In Strength. Rogues might dump a few extra points in Dexterity due to their evasive nature.

Each score has a modifier attached to it, the number that's applied to a die roll when a character tries to do something related to that ability. If your DM asks you to perform an ability check before performing an action like picking a lock or swimming across a lake or faking your way into an embassy function, you'll simply roll your twenty-sided die and add the appropriate modifier (positive or negative) from your character sheet. The DM will compare your number to the target number and let you know if you have succeeded.

Poor Jak. Our clumsy rogue often attempts things his rogue counterparts can do with their rapiers tied behind their backs. He once tried jumping from one horse-drawn carriage to another and tumbled himself right into a ditch. Ouch. On another occasion he jumped into a 30-foot crevice with a 40-foot rope. If Jak was a cartoon character he'd constantly have a bevy of birdies swarming over his head. Dexterous or not, Jak certainly has . . . excuse the pun . . . character.

Astrid's ability scores (at level 5):

Ability	Ability Score	Modifier
Strength	11	0
Dexterity	16	+3
Constitution	10	0
Intelligence	15	+2
Wisdom	14	+2
Charisma	17	+3

Ursula's ability scores (at level 5):

Ability	Ability Score	Modifier
Strength	16	+3
Dexterity	12	+1
Constitution	18	+4
Intelligence	14	+2
Wisdom	14	+2
Charisma	5	−3

Check out the differences between Ursula and Astrid. Ursula may have the Charisma of a brick but she's brawny as a brick house. And Astrid would probably break a sweat opening a checking account but she can sweet-talk free passage on a train with a wink and a hair toss. Besides, who doesn't love an elf? That's why it's important to have a well-rounded D&D group. And like your real group of friends, you make concessions for each other. Never let the contentious one talk her way out of a speeding ticket, for instance. And try not to let your buddy who's so weak she can't break a nail be the first to enter an abandoned building. On second thought, don't let any of your friends enter an abandoned building.

I know Astrid is fragile. I've come to terms with that. It might even explain why she dresses like a Vegas showgirl. But I believe in accentuating the positive, and my baby is riddled with plus signs. Astrid's got skills. Mad, crazy, magical skills. Come on! You know you've wished for this special ability. An evil glare that could cause an asteroid to plummet through the sky, burning up the softball field just as you were about to take a swing. You're late for a hair appointment and if you don't get that green light, your partial foil is liable to default to a walk-in bang trim. If only the monster Cadillac would pick up the pace you'd be in good shape but alas—no such luck. The light turns red and you sprout more of the grays you're trying to cover up. Wouldn't it be cool to cast a hovercraft spell on your vehicle and bypass the bypass? Heck yeah!

Check Yourself Before You Wreck Yourself

The "much more" I was referencing above means your character's other statistics. Don't worry, they're easily located on the front page of the character sheet and once you fill them out the first time, they only increase in numbers small enough you don't need two hands to add them up.

Initiative Modifier: This number is added to your die roll to determine who goes first in combat. Basically, the higher this number, the more likely you'll be the appetizer before the entrée. When your DM says, "roll for initiative," roll your twenty-sided die and if you're a wimp like me, pray for a low number.

Speed: Get ye olde arses back on those treadmills. This number is the Presidential Fitness Award to a D&D character. This number tells how far your character can move (in feet) in a round of play.

Attack and Damage Modifiers: Sure, you'd like to believe you'd know exactly what to do if some lunatic jumped out of that van your mom told you never to park next to, but would you? These numbers represent your weapon of choice, what you need to roll to attack the lunatic, and how much damage you'll inflict when you do. (P.S.: Mom says to always keep a roll of quarters in your purse so you'll do some serious damage when swatting at the bad guys. I say that's just an additional ten bucks you'll lose after you drop your purse and run faster than a bride-to-be at Filene's Basement bridal gown sale.)

Armor Class (or AC): This number is what the lunatic in the van needs to roll to hit you during combat.

Hit Points: This number represents how much pain and misery your character can withstand during wedding season—I mean combat. What's the difference really? The higher the number, the thicker your skin. The lower the number, the more likely you're a Pisces or haven't finished going

Want to live long and prosper in the D&D universe? Play an elf who on average doesn't clock out until around 700 years.

The following races have these (above) average life spans:

Elves: 700 years   Gnomes: 500 years
Dwarves: 700 years   Halflings: 250 years
Humans: barely touching the century mark

through puberty yet. When your hit points hit 0, you're the D&D equivalent of hiding under the duvet, watching *Grease 2* and snuggling with the only men who will ever love you again—Ben and Jerry.

Probably the most important number to your character is his or her level, or the measure of your character's power in the game. Obviously a 6th-level character is more powerful than a 5th-level character and with each advancement, your character becomes stronger and gains new abilities. You will start the game as a 1st-level character.

Leveling up requires know-how. Another wonderful aspect of D&D is that experience gets you power, not a reputation. You gain experience points (or XP) when your character overcomes challenges, such as putting the smack down on an evil oversized rodent or unearthing a long-lost scroll and returning it to its rightful owner. Each level's advancement requires a certain amount of experience points. Astrid advanced to 2nd level after only 1,000 points (about three D&D sessions). It was a proud moment, my little Astrid, advancing to the next level. I felt like taking her and her friends out to Pizza Hut to celebrate the big moment and then shopping for the new spells she was allowed to learn. My mini was growing up so fast!

Finding My Inner Elf

When Teddy handed me my fully filled-out character sheet and my mini, I couldn't help but feel a little bit proud. Cradling my mini me in the palm of my hand, I realized that D&D isn't just a game—it's a lesson in DNA. I made—okay, Teddy made—a new life. I secretly hoped that my alter ego would possess the brains of a NASA engineer and have the body of a Victoria's Secret model, but thanks to a spin of the old wheel of genetics I'm a busty, lithe blonde elf sorcerer with Tina Turner thighs and a Cher-like wardrobe. That'll work. My girl is above average in Intelligence and Charisma, knows a handful of cool spells, and would really make a better spectator than athlete when it comes to the wide world of weaponry. I hope she knows how to duck.

Astrid comes alive!

"I shall call her Astrid," I said, petting her long, blonde hair with my index finger.

"You can call her whatever you want," Teddy said. "She's yours."

Racial Profiling

While there are several races to choose from in the world of *Dungeons & Dragons*, the following are the most popular. Don't worry; you can still be a human if the thought of playing a gnome conjures up images of creepy, ubiquitous garden dwellers.

Dwarf: Dwarves are generally short, stocky, and super tough. They probably played on the college softball team and grew up to be gym teachers. They throw kick-ass parties where they serve Jell-O shots and still drink out of red plastic cups. Dressing up means wearing socks. They are known to vacation in Denver. Play a dwarf if you enjoy beating up people, have a courageous spirit, and favor dark, dank sewers for adventuring.

Elf: Elves are hot. Okay, maybe I'm biased. Or maybe Orlando Bloom rocks a pair of pointy ears better than most. Elves are creative, graceful, and have a penchant for spellcasting. Standing about 5-1/2 feet tall, they have average in-seams, which means they seldom need to have their pants hemmed. Elves have been spotted vacationing in Ashland, Oregon during the Shakespeare festival. Play an elf if *The Witches of Eastwick* inspired you, you have a flair for individuality, or if you look good in tights.

Gnome: If a gnome invites you for dinner, go. They're known for over-indulging and if they go down into a vortex of hedonistic debauchery, they're taking you with them. Gnomes are related to dwarves but are like the lucky cousins who grew up without a curfew and ate organic fruit and were allowed to watch R-rated movies. They're also extremely short at only 3-1/2 feet tall, which makes carrying them home after a long night of partying easy. They have a timeshare in Cabo San Lucas and hate to see it go to waste.

Halfling: Halflings were most likely gymnasts in a past life. They're small and muscular and incessantly perky. When not practicing triple back-spring aerials off high beams, they can be found polishing their fossil collections and figuring out a way to make their appliances solar powered. They do not take vacations. They make pilgrimages. Play a halfling if you've never lived in one place for the duration of your lease, won more than a hundred dollars on a lottery ticket, or have ever been told "sorry, we don't have your size."

Half-elf: Half-elves are good people. They're charismatic, clever, curious, and were voted most likely to do a bunch of things after high school. Half-elves were the kids who would do anything. They grew up eating mud, ringing the doorbells of the oldest and scariest ladies on the block, and asking the hottest girls in school to the prom. Half-elves break into beach houses in the winter and invite their friends to stay with them. Play a half-elf if you think you might be crazy, enjoy breaking and entering, or have ever been tasked with doing something because no one else wanted to.

Human: Humans come in many shapes and sizes in the world of D&D. Pretend every conniving, over-qualified, MBA-toting contestant on *The Apprentice* was a race all his or her own. There. That's a human in the world of D&D. Play a human if you like learning new tasks and being rewarded for it, are adaptable and well rounded, or have ever seriously considered auditioning for *The Apprentice*.

Have Some Class

Now that you've chosen your character's race, it's time to choose your class from the gazillion that are offered. At the risk of sending you into anxiety-ridden SAT flashbacks, we'll again cover some of the classics . . . okay, the ones I know best. For a more extensive list, check out the *Player's Handbook*.

Class is essentially your character's major except it's a field he or she will actually go into after college and might even get paid for it.

Fighter: As Patty Smyth once sang, I am the warrior! Patty would probably play this character. The fighter is the first into battle, the one who yells *"Stand back!"* before realizing the rest of you have already locked yourselves in the bathroom. Your fighter friends are the ones into martial arts, rugby, and drinking Chivas Regal out of a dirty soccer cleat.

FEELING RACY

It's true, we've been taught to never choose one race over another, but in D&D it's a necessary evil. If your moral compass won't point in one direction or another, then take the following quiz and blame it on your psychological make-up.

1. You are being forced to try out of a reality television show. You audition for:
   a. *Survivor*
   b. *Project Runway*
   c. *Last Comic Standing*
   d. *Big Brother*
   e. What do you mean *forced*? I sent my tape in ages ago.

2. When relaxing you:
   a. Visit your masseuse Brutus for some deep tissue lovin'
   b. Write in your journal
   c. Think of clever places to leave whoopee cushions for your co-workers
   d. Shoplift
   e. Take a personality quiz in a magazine

3. To you, success is:
   a. Making your mother proud
   b. Getting out of a rut
   c. Finding a late 4th-century Scythian gold belt buckle at a garage sale
   d. Paying off your credit cards
   e. Getting a callback for a reality television show

4. Your best friend is someone who:
   a. Makes you laugh by putting whoopee cushions on your co-workers chairs
   b. Is very much like yourself
   c. Laughs at your jokes
   d. Just got a callback for a reality television show
   e. You met in kindergarten

5. You would date someone based solely on their:
   a. Credit score
   b. Ability to recite Christopher Marlowe
   c. Tell a joke
   d. Drop serious amounts of coin
   e. Promote you

6. The Commodores say she's a brick house. They'd think you were a:
   a. Brick
   b. Elegant, graceful skyscraper
   c. Yurt
   d. Shanty on the shore
   e. Four bedrooms, three bath split level in the suburbs

AND NOW FOR THE RESULTS

Mostly A's: Look around—are there six more little ones just like you? Do any of them go by Doc, Dopey, or Dummy? Have you ever covertly housed a friend on the lam and ended up doing all the cooking and cleaning while she goes catting around with her Prince Charming? You're definitely bent toward the dwarf persuasion.

Mostly B's: Remember the little Polly Pee Pee dolly and circus animal train set you poo poo'd that Christmas when you were four? How would you feel knowing your ancestors worked their pointy shoes into the snow slaving over that for you? That's right, teepee ears, you're a hoity-toity elf.

Mostly C's: Do you often close your eyes only to wake up in a different place? Do you find it difficult to reach the contents on the top shelf of your medicine cabinet? Have you ever been ticketed by the fashion police for wearing a ridiculously tall, pointy, bright red hat in public? Why don't you find a nice set of shrubs to chill out under and think about your new life as a gnome.

Mostly D's: Do you like zebras, moon cookies, and minotaurs? Sometimes feel like a nut? Maybe sometimes don't? Were you born under the sign of Gemini? Maybe you like heads and tails, right and left, black and white. Or maybe you should play a halfling.

Mostly E's: Surprise! You're a . . . you! Why be a 3 -1/2-foot-tall lawn ornament or be resigned to wearing stupid hats when you could just be . . . you! Way to step out of your comfort zone. The best thing about playing a human in the world of D&D is that you're automatically about a thousand degrees cooler than a human in the real world.

Rogue: Who hasn't encountered a rogue or two? Cunning little bastards—sorry. Wrong book. The rogue is the guy in high school who chalked IDs and turned fifteen-year-old babysitters into twenty-eight-year-old baby mamas. The rogue picks a lock with his Amex card and

HEAD OF THE CLASS

If opposites aren't attracting you or you're torn between two classes, take the following quiz to determine which class best suits you.

1. You've won a dream vacation. Your bags are packed for:
   A. A desert spa get-away for some serious pampering
   B. A twelve-day trek through the Andes mountains
   C. Destination unknown, you'll know when you get there
   D. Boot camp

2. Your best friend just got dumped. You:
   A. Tell her she's beautiful and smart and much better without the lowlife scumbag and give her enough margaritas until she believes you
   B. Take the strand of hair and old shoelace you stole from his car and plant it along with an eye of newt in a hole in your backyard
   C. Wait for him to leave for work and peg him with multicolored spit wads
   D. Kick his ass

3. Your most expensive splurge was:
   A. A pair of Manolo Blahniks
   B. A kayak
   C. Night vision goggles and a nanny cam
   D. A sensei

4. In social situations you:
   A. Mix and a' mingle
   B. Show slides of your latest adventure
   C. Pick pockets
   D. Are often asked to not come back. Ever.

continued on next page

uses his charm to avoid paying late fees. He's the kid who followed you to school making fart noises, told everyone you slept with a teddy bear and a nightlight, and copied your math homework. You probably had a crush on him.

5. Alcohol gives you:
   A. Beer muscles
   B. A handy disinfectant
   C. Easy prey
   D. A reason to get up in the morning

6. If forced to help out your community, you would:
   A. Tutor kids after school
   B. Pick up litter
   C. Move
   D. Teach self-defense classes

7. If a fight broke out next to you, you would:
   A. Get the hell out of the way. The sight of blood makes you queasy, especially the sight of blood on your new shoes.
   B. Get your first-aid kit from the car and wait on the sidelines for the loser
   C. Be at the center of it
   D. Have thrown the first punch

RESULTS

Mostly A's: If you answered mostly A's you should start your D&D life as a sorcerer or a cleric. If you answered A to question seven, you're probably inclined toward the sorcerer persuasion. B would lean toward a cleric.

Mostly B's: If you answered mostly B's, you and Chuck Norris are what fine rangers are made of.

Mostly C's: Mostly C's sees you as a rogue.

Mostly D's: Mostly D's would imply you've got some anger management issues. Oh, and you'd make a great fighter.

Sorcerer: Or sometimes a sorceress, if she wants to make her gender absolutely clear. Regardless of how they prefer to address themselves, sorcerers are real charmers! Sorcerers often have striking good looks (see page 51 of the *Player's Handbook* if you don't believe me). They may not have the chops of a mama bear when it comes to battle, but they share the grizzly's instinct when it comes to protecting their friends. She's a lover, not a fighter, so if faced with combat she'll most likely cast *bitch slap* and stand there with her eyes scrunched shut, praying her tougher friends come to the rescue. Calling on magical spells, the sorcerer is the quiet *fireball*-wielding diva. She's the type of girl who makes her own Christmas cards but will stab you in the throat with her fabric shears if you look at her wrong.

Cleric: Clerics rely on magic and divine inspiration to help them out of tough spots. The cleric is your best pal, the one who knows exactly what to say to make you feel better. When the cleric says "Forget it, you were too good for him anyway," you believe her. When she tells you the cut of the pants you're wearing are very slimming, you buy them in every color. Clerics are an asset to every group because of their ability to cast healing and protective spells. They've got a decent left hook, too.

Ranger: Rangers are the rogues of the wild. They are shifty little tree huggers with badass warrior tendencies. They're quick-footed, which is quite the accomplishment considering most are probably wearing Birkenstocks. They dropped out of college to follow Phish on tour and work on their conspiracy theories. Rangers are weird, but they're handier to your team than a Swiss army knife. It's not nice to fool Mother Nature because rangers are mama's boys.

There are lots of other classes to choose from. Take a gander through the *Player's Handbook* or visit one of the websites mentioned previously to see what else is out there.

· ·

Group Therapy

My group gets together weekly in a freezing teleconference room with fluorescent lights that incessantly buzz overhead. We have come together in this very room several times before to discuss ad campaigns, marketing strategies, and inventory reports. But on Mondays we meet as rogues, rangers, fighters, and clerics to discuss how we've ended up in Sharn, the City of Towers, and how the heck we're going to get out alive. I guess it's not surprising we gravitate toward characters very unlike ourselves.

I'm pretty positive that none of us could save a princess if she came with her own lid-locking Tupperware system. And yuck. Who'd want to? Princesses have become so tedious and annoying. A dog or a pastry chef or someone who could get tickets to an Oprah taping would be more motivating.

Petite and sweet Lucy chose to play a stocky dwarf in need of a lip wax and manicure. Armando, the nicest guy on the block, plays a rugged rogue. He, like most of us, probably harbors secret dreams of slaying the dragon but in reality has a hard time making his black lab sit on command. Calvin, who sits in the emergency exits on airplanes because he wants to be the first one out, wanted to play a healing and protecting cleric. It's not entirely surprising Hank chose to play a half-elf ranger. He's an avid outdoorsman who enjoys fly-fishing, bird hunting, and debunking other people's conspiracy theories. But he's not weird and I've never seen him in Birkenstocks. Helena is most like her character. She chose something complicated like a shifter, a unique race having the ability to take on animalistic features, to prove she's smarter than everyone. She probably would have skipped middle school but didn't want to graduate college before she was legally allowed to buy the champagne to celebrate.

I'm not a therapist (nor, much to my mother's dismay, in therapy) but it doesn't take a Dr. Phil knock-off to figure out that DUNGEONS & DRAGONS gives players a creative license to be someone they've always wanted to be—and not in a Single White Female sort of way. When I ran my theory by an avid D&D fan and confessed I thought my character was so much cooler than the real me, he simply said, "Duh." Duh indeed. If you're going to have an alter ego, shouldn't she be the new and improved you? Why order the regular when the super-sized you is only ten cents more?

Are You a Good Witch or a Bad Witch?

There is a scene in the Wizard of Oz that's always irked me. Dorothy lands in a new world all dazed and confused and runs into Glinda's glowing orb. Glinda laughs off Dorothy's "are you or aren't you" question by saying something like "Duh, Dorothy, bad witches are wicked ugly and clearly I'm a ravishing beauty," and *then* proceeds to ask Dorothy if she is a good witch or a bad witch. What is Glinda implying about the naïve little farm girl with a concussion? "Gee, Dorothy, blue gingham is kind of dated and those pigtails might have been cute twelve years ago and for the love of Oz, dogs were given four legs for a reason. Take the mutt out of the picnic basket and let him see why it's called the Yellow Brick Road." She may have been a good witch, but I always found Glinda a bit patronizing and catty. And if she was going to knock anything, it should have been Dorothy's bobby socks and patent leather shoes.

In the world of DUNGEONS & DRAGONS, good and evil often confound your character. Good and evil go beyond the basics you learned in Sunday school. They are embedded in the earth your character walks on, the air she breathes, the stars that shine down at night. We're talking Sunday brunch buffet with fruit *and* fondue. How do you choose?

How your character would choose depends on her alignment. There are almost as many alignments as there are Kabbalah bracelets in Hollywood. Rest assured none of these alignments will wind up on the "so five minutes ago" list anytime soon. Your character's race and/or class can sometimes determine your alignment. In other cases, it simply influences your choice. Alignments are comprised of good, evil, lawful, and chaotic. There are nine alignments total but only six that apply to player characters. The remaining three are for monsters and bad guys.

Bust out the incense, cleanse your chakra, and open your third eye. It's time to choose your alignment.

Lawful Good: As you might expect, lawful good characters are sugar and spice and everything nice. They fight against evil and want to see wrongdoers get punished. If they had their way, grocery stores would tar and feather anyone who snuck sixteen items into the fifteen-items-or-less express lane. A lawful good character might be a goody-two-shoes but she would also keep your dirty, dark secret for all of eternity. Unless that was you in the express lane.

Lawful Good Celeb: Picture a star who could remove her toenail polish with hundred-dollar bills if she were someone who actually took care of her own toes. This person hates to see nurses and lunch ladies go without cashmere hoodies and MP3 players. If she's feeling frisky, she might buy you and 349 of your neighbors a brand new Pontiac. But watch it—if she's feeling wronged, she won't think twice about outing you on national television. Don't mess with a lawful good celeb.

Neutral Good: Neutral good characters believe in being the best they can be without getting all up in the bad guy's business. A neutral good character will be the first to offer to bring a dessert to the party and the one who stays last to help clean up. They're committed to helping others but leave the punishing to the pros. They wouldn't want to upset the balance of order.

Neutral Good Celeb: Being a neutral good character doesn't just involve good character. A billion dollar bank account, some cool shades, and an accent so smooth it could be spread on toast always helps. Anyone can write a check with armies of zeroes attached, but not everyone will get the hem of their Versace jeans dirty trying to make a difference. Spending quality time with the stuffy suits in DC and stuffy suites in the African desert isn't everyone's idea of a good time, especially if a media makeover isn't your MO. Neutral good celebs don't just see wrongdoing, they want to do right.

Chaotic Good: Chaotic good characters are under the influence of their conscience. Stealing from the rich and giving to the poor is only one item on their ever-increasing rap sheet. Their hearts are in the right place, but the road to get them there is often paved with blackballs and warrants for their arrests. Forever in the underdogs' camp, the chaotic good character was the kid on the playground who bullied the bullies.

Chaotic Good Celeb: Anyone associated with PETA. Sure, poking and prodding little baby bunnies is mean, but dousing fur-clad humans with fake blood and stripping down to your own furless, surgically enhanced birthday suits won't make it stop. Idealistic teenagers appreciate the effort and the bunnies probably would too if they knew what was going on in their honor, but the ladies who lunch and the pimp daddies probably don't give a turd.

Lawful Neutral: Lawful neutral characters have political aspirations. Why else would they be so law-abiding and moral? Acting under a strong desire for order and organization, lawful neutral characters remain unswayed by opponents on either side. They're dedicated to their cause without being pushy.

Lawful Neutral Celeb: Any host or company member involved in children's television. Whether you're an animated, absurd-looking animal mutation or a colorful suspender-tugging, glassy eyed, sing-alonging grown up, you're as neutral as khakis as long as you're a good friend and role model who doesn't know enough to be condescending. Lawful neutral types know what they know and will gladly impart that knowledge. And they're not afraid to ask the big questions like "Why can't we all just get along?"

Neutral: The neutral character is the liberal arts major of the D&D universe. They see good and evil, law and chaos—but instead of choosing a side, they straddle the line in the middle because they see the danger of going to extremes. Neutrals are noncommittal and bored by controversy. They're not wishy-washy or even pushovers, but they will probably be the first to jump on the bandwagon and get off a block later.

Neutral Celeb: There's a ton of these "I'm With the Bandwagon" celebs all eating at the same restaurants, wearing the same designers, getting the same cup sizes from the same ultra-discreet plastic surgeons. Boring. You don't get on the cover of *Us Weekly* getting busted for peeking under every rock from Hollywood to Bollywood trying to find an identity to call your own. Confused? Maybe. Neutral? Likely. Working with an A-list publicist who is going to ditch your conformist ass unless you accidentally show a nipple or sleep with your neighbor's nanny? *Us Weekly* and I hope so.

Chaotic Neutral: You know those guests who pass around inappropriate dinnertime topics like they were chicken wrapped in bacon? That's why you invite them, isn't it? The chaotic neutral player is the stuff clichés are made of. Think before you speak. March to the beat of your own drummer. He's all about what's right for him and making that right for you. He doesn't dispute authority—he pretends it doesn't exist. Chaotic neutral characters are unpredictable and overzealous and probably carry pamphlets describing their latest craze on them at all time just in case you're dying of boredom in a stalled elevator somewhere.

Chaotic Neutral Celeb: Better move the coffee table and cover your couch in plastic should this celeb stop by. Yeah, we know they're *very* into religion. We know they know how to negotiate a killer contract. We get that prescription drugs are a no-no in their book. What they don't get is what's good for the goose is not necessarily good for the gander. Not on my couch, you don't!

Baby's Got Back ... Story

I may regret admitting I gave my stuffed animals marriage licenses and torrid sexual pasts if no one admits they did it too. Anyone? No? Fine. Fortunately for me, the world of DUNGEONS & DRAGONS encourages this sort of behavior. What good is an alter ego without a shady past? Or a promising future? The dice may have a hand in your character's present, but you control your character's past. Maybe your dwarf has dabbled in diamond heists. Maybe your rogue is an aspiring watercolor artist who studied his craft under the greatest masters of his time. Maybe your ranger is a veterinarian or a sheep farmer or maybe she makes her own line of expensive t-shirts that celebrities can't do without. Maybe your elf harbors secret desires to be a dentist but his parents are forcing him into the family toy-building business. All right, that one's been done before, but you get the picture.

If Astrid is a blank white wall and my mind is a projector, she's about to take on all the tasks I haven't gotten around to. Not in this life, anyway. Here's what I can tell you about Astrid Bellagio:

She was born one hundred and thirty-four years ago into incredible wealth and opportunity. She has an older brother and two older sisters who adore her even though Astrid is clearly her parents' favorite. Her father is the sole proprietor of an exclusive and tastefully decorated inn and casino popular with human nobles. Her mother is a famous diplomat and professor of spellcasting. Astrid was a spellcasting prodigy, breezing through magic school several decades before her peers. With all that free time, the ever-ambitious Astrid decided to learn a few more crafts. When she's not chasing down lost treasure and wayward vampires, she works at a marine biology facility off the coast of St. Thomas where she rehabs sick dolphins and makes friends with those just passing by. She's the best dolphin trainer in the country, possibly in the world. Yes, in fact, the world. When she's not healing the flippers she's studying to become an astronaut. She also writes children's books and helms an international cosmetic company. She invented chocolate that speeds up your metabolism. If you combine it with peanut butter you instantly lose five pounds. She also stars on a popular day-time soap, dates a rock star, and runs a convalescent home for senior dogs. She speaks several languages including Draconic, Goblin, and Italian. She is a talented piano player and lounge singer and designs a high-end line of wedding dresses. Easily bored, Astrid often seeks adventure and moving targets she can sic her *magic missiles* on. Her best friend is Ursula.

Phew. I'm exhausted. I may cancel that knitting class after all. Who has the time for it? (Okay, so maybe I got a little carried away. Most of that stuff doesn't exist in the D&D universe. Whose fantasy life is it, anyway?) Now that you have the background and the basics for creating your own character, dive into the dice bag and see what D&DNA has in store for you.

Game On!

Finally it's time to get the Monday night party started. We're no longer co-workers and boring old humans in various levels of employment. We're a band of merry adventurers with various levels of skills, strength, and smarts. I'm sitting at a table where an hour ago I was watching a vendor pitch the merits of his printing facility. Now I sit watching Teddy set the stage for what will be our first official game. He does math and shuffles cards behind a screen, reads his notes intently, wipes down play mats and draws new, intensely detailed maps on them with shrubs and walkways. Now I know why his fingers are always tinted in some marker shade of blue or green. We chat while we wait for Teddy to finish up, conversation ranging from rising interest rates to changes in our 401K plans to potty-training techniques. Ancient lore dictates we should be blowing Doritos dust off our dice and the only rising interest in a D&D group should be in comic books. Potty talk is probably timeless.

I don't know if it's the scent of his markers or all the math I'm about to do, but I'm lost already. Too bad the make-believe city of Sharn isn't serviced by On-Star.

Before we can send our characters on their first adventure, we need to make sure they've got the right gear. Teddy sets the stage for us.

"You've come to a large piazza. Shrub-shrouded sidewalks lead to shops supplying food, armor, and weapons."

"We're in a mall?" I ask, easily getting into character. So far this role-playing thing isn't so challenging.

"No," Teddy says. "It's outside."

"Lots of malls are outside," I say.

"Fashion Valley Mall in San Diego is one of the nicest outdoor malls in the country," Calvin says. Hank looks disappointed that his friend would know this.

"I love Fashion Valley," Lucy says. "I haven't shopped in so long."

"Fine," Teddy says. "You're in a mall."

"Let's go! Let's go!" I say, as our minis charge through Fashion Valley Piazza. "It's the Nordstrom half-yearly sale!"

"Why would I charge for that?" Calvin asks. "It's for women and children only."

"We can make it be for men too," I offer, and then realize I may be stepping on the Dungeon Master's toes. "I mean, if Teddy says it's okay."

Teddy and Helena simultaneously roll their eyes. She'd cast "Get a life" on the whole room if she could.

"Can we stop at the food court?" Hank asks. "I'm starving."

"You're metagaming again," accuses Helena, the roleplaying police.

"Fine. Can Yakama stop at the food court? He's starving."

"There is no food court," Teddy explains. "It's the Middle Ages."

"There is too a food court," Calvin says. "They even have a Cheesecake Factory."

"I love Cheesecake Factory," Lucy says. "Let's go there."

Teddy puts down his pencil and picks up a Tom Clancy novel. He crosses one leg over the other and settles into where he left off.

Armando, who until this point has remained as neutral as tofu in a stir-fry, is concerned. "I think we're pissing off the Dungeon Master and it's probably not a good idea to do that. He is in control of our fate, after all." Aside from Helena, Armando is the only member of our group who has played D&D before. But in the true spirit of DUNGEONS & DRAGONS, he wants to go with the group decision. If we're okay with pissing off Teddy, so is he.

"The dice are in control of your fate," Teddy says, not looking up from the page. "Not me."

"Now who's metagaming?" I say which makes no sense but I really like tossing the word *metagaming* around. I'm going to think of a way to incorporate it into all my conversations.

"That's not metagaming," says Helena.

Scratch that—work it into every conversation that doesn't include Helena, who obviously has the power to shift herself into a glossary.

META-MOUTH

Let's get back to this metagaming business because it will probably haunt you. As Teddy describes it, roleplaying means, "you listen to the Dungeon Master and decide what your character does based on his or her strengths, weaknesses, and personality. Metagaming is asking the Dungeon Master a question and watching his face to see if he's hiding anything." For instance, upon learning of a secret doorway in a dingy old dungeon with odd shaped footprints leading up to it, Astrid might say something like "Let's check this out. I've got a light source and I'm number one!" Astrid's mommy might say something like, "Doesn't Astrid see those footprints? Doesn't she know something is hiding in there? Is she stupid?" Hey, you spent all that time creating a character, it's only natural you'd want to protect her. But if you know something your character doesn't, don't let it influence the game.

"How about we think of a way to make it up to Teddy over a piece of peanut butter and toffee cheesecake?" Lucy asks.

"I don't eat cheesecake," Teddy says, eyes still on the page. "Lactose intolerant."

Helena is angry. She takes her mini monk off the play mat and begins packing up her handbooks. "We're supposed to be playing D&D, not planning a happy hour."

"No one said anything about happy hour," Calvin says.

"But now that she did. . . ." Lucy says. Her eyes are red from lack of sleep, making her look like she's already had a few hours of happiness.

"Helena's right," Hank says, which makes my ears bleed. "Teddy doesn't have all day. Let's go back to the piazza. We can get cheesecake later."

Helena shoots me a one of those "I smell something sour" smirks and shrugs her shoulders with false modesty. I'm not even the one who wanted cheesecake! Rewind twenty-five years ago and there she is racing down my sidewalk with Beauty Secrets Barbie in one hand and a fistful of polyester blonde hair in the other. I laugh at the thought.

"Fine," Calvin says. "Instead of Cheesecake Factory it can be Ye Olde Mead and Ale Factory. But we should still get a good meal in. It's important to keep our metabolism up."

I'm pretty sure Amok isn't training for a triathlon and I could use my new favorite word and call metagaming again, but I don't. It's important for me to keep my metabolism up too. At least that's what I rationalize as I squash another handful of Kashi into my mouth.

Teddy bookmarks his page and asks us if we're sure; he doesn't get much time to read these days and was really getting into the book. Convinced, he begins to spin the tale of murder, intrigue, and mystery. We are enjoying an evening stroll through Fashion Valley Piazza when rain begins pounding down, making it hard to see.

"Oh no!" I say, hoping Astrid's purple cloak has a magic hood tucked inside.

Teddy continues in his camp counselor voice. "The lanterns lighting the paths barely illuminate a few feet ahead of you. Everyone, give me a Spot check."

What Teddy is asking us to do is roll a twenty-sided die and add the die's total to the number under "Spot" in the skill section of your character sheet. You're basically finding out what, if anything, your character sees that could help you make a decision about what to do. If you roll high, you're probably very observant and caught a clue. If you roll low, you were probably digging lip gloss out of the bottom of your purse and missed the whole thing.

"Seven," I say, giving Teddy my total.

Teddy shakes his head, giving me an "I don't think so" look.

"Astrid was too busy pulling gum off her heels to notice anything," Hank offers.

"Maybe she was busy undressing Amok with her eyes," Calvin suggests.

"Maybe she's nearsighted," Lucy says. "It's okay."

But it's not okay because I feel very let down. Doesn't Astrid remember anything I told her about minding her surroundings? In no time she'll be duct-taped in the back of a van with two derelicts claiming they wanted to smell her perfume. I check to see if common sense is a skill choice so I can dump all my points there.

"Twenty-four," Helena says. What I hear is *You people suck.* Everyone else's scores range from twelve to nineteen.

Teddy gets all camp counselor on us again. "All right, Tenoctris and Yakama notice a cloaked figure moving in the dark, seemingly making an effort to avoid the dim pools of light."

Everyone seems sufficiently impressed by this except me. It's a mall. Why is it weird to see someone walking around?

"Lightning flashes," Teddy continues. "And you notice a shape on the cobblestones. The shadowy figure slips over the railing and into the night."

Armando does that "Dunt, dunt, dunt" sound, like an organ in a bad B movie. It's inevitable that someone does this during every encounter.

I feel like I just stepped into a *Melrose Place* rerun, which makes me giddy with glee. It takes about an entire episode's time to decide if we should call the police or go after the shadowy silhouettes ourselves. Where's Heather Locklear when you need her?

Okay, maybe this is more ADD than D&D but you get the gist. Right? Fear not. The following chapters will lay it all out for you and your pals. And remember, if you're not having fun, you're breaking a very important rule.

Dear Diary,

Ever have one of those days when you wish you were somebody else? I'm having one today. Why oh why did I have to be born with these super-special magical skills? My mom says it's an inborn talent and there's nothing I can do about it. I didn't choose magic, it chose me. Yadda, yadda, yadda. Daddy once told me some sorcerers believe dragon's blood is in our veins. Maybe that explains why I feel like a flaming bitch sometimes. Anyway, my friend Ursula is a fighter. She's trained all her life to be a fighter. She won't cop to it, but I know she's got a few regulars who will pay her to get a job done on their behalf. She's pretty hush hush about these things, and once she even said it was better if I didn't know. I let it drop, of course. I mean, I do watch The Sopranos after all.

I'm sure Ursula would think it was cool to magically send secret messages to anyone who is asleep or charm a monster into believing it's your ally, just like I think it would be cool to drop kick an ogre in my ballet flats or unstick the lid to a jar of honey after it hardens in your cabinet for a year. Ursula is pretty badass. She's also a dwarf, which makes her pretty short. She may be able to open the jar of honey, but she certainly couldn't reach it. And as pretty as she is, her calves are so freakin' huge, she'd never be able to find tall boots to zip over them. I guess being an elf has its advantages, like a long graceful build and no facial hair. Saves me a fortune on eyebrow waxings. And I could always be a socially challenged monk with a major chip on my shoulder like Tenoctris. Oh dear, I just got a bad case of the willies. Okay, maybe life isn't so bad after all. Besides, there has to be a spell out there to open sticky jars, right?

Love, Astrid

GREATSWORD— DON'T LEAVE HOME WITHOUT IT

If *DUNGEONS & DRAGONS* had a fashion rag, it would recommend that your character always be equipped with the following items:

 A melee weapon such as a sword or dagger

 A ranged weapon such as a bow or crossbow

 Class-appropriate armor

 A shield (for clerics and fighters)

 Class-specific items such as a holy symbol or thieves' tools

 Light sources such as torches and lanterns

 Tindertwigs (or matches)

 A backpack

Food rations

Wish: Forget wishful thinking. Cast this spell and they're all yours.

Chapter Three
WILL WORK FOR MASTERWORK ARMOR

Got a little jingle in your pocket? That's the sound of gold and silver pieces eagerly awaiting some serious spendage. Now that you have your character and your character has a purpose, it's time for what I deem the most important part of the game: shopping.

Starting a D&D adventure with a new character is much like starting middle school with a backpack full of sharpened pencils, a scientific calculator, and a brand spanking new Trapper Keeper.

This I can do. This is where I will outshine my fellow players. Surely I could rocket through a few hundred levels with my bargain-hunting prowess. Unfortunately, Target doesn't carry holy symbols or crossbows.

Until now, dressing for battle meant putting preemptive Band-Aids on my heels before slipping into my favorite, albeit ill-fitting shoes. In the land of dungeon delving, it means outfitting your character with proper equipment—the kind of proper equipment you'd expect to see in a hunting lodge deep in the bowels of Nothingness, North Dakota. Actually, scratch that. You'd never expect to see this.

And now for the proverbial monsoon over your shopping parade, we need to talk money. You need to know what you're spending before you can spend it, right? Isn't that what your parents taught you when you came of age and the creditors started soliciting you? Even though D&D is steeped in fantasy, it's still a world that needs money to make it go round and round. I know—major buzz kill.

Gold Digging

The common currency in D&D consists of gold, silver, and copper pieces, or gp, sp, and cp respectively. For example, if a manicure and pedicure costs 5 gp, that's 5 gold pieces and really freakin' expensive for a mani-pedi. Try one of those quickie walk-in joints attached to every strip mall.

Generally every character starts off with enough money to buy basic gear. You'll earn more money along the way and if you choose to spend it on a new crossbow or rock hammer, that's fine. (By the way, if you choose to spend money on designer shoes, that's okay too. Says who? Says me, that's who.)

When choosing your gear, don't forget to check out your racial advantages. For example, elves are automatically proficient with the longsword and shortbow (among other weapons), so it makes sense to carry them. Unless, of course, your weapon of choice is a Fendi bag full of pepper spray. Elves are accomplished accessorizers as well.

The D&D rulebooks make it easy to gear up for adventure by offering every class a starting package consisting of equipment appropriate to your character's class. If you choose to handpick your goods, you purchase items *a la carte* with a random number of gold pieces determined by your character's class. I'm not a risk taker when it comes to money. I don't even like buying things on clearance if it means final sale. But I do like buying things, so I opted to buy Astrid's gear item by item. Doing so means the dice once again determine my fate, this time the fate of my bank statement. Random starting gold for your class is determined by rolling a four-sided die, multiplying that number by a predetermined number, and multiplying again by ten. Huh? I hear you. Bear with me.

Average starting gold for a sorcerer is 75 gp (compared to the moneybag ranger at 150 gp and the very financially challenged monk who only has 12 gp to play with). But that's the average. The dice could put your total above or below your fellow classmates. To determine the wealth of your character, you'll be faced with a cryptic formula like this:

Sorcerers roll 3d4 x 10.

Don't panic. This is not a test. I repeat, this is not a test. That means, I roll a four-sided die three times and multiply that total by ten to come up with my bank statement. Sure easier than managing my 401K plan. My first tumble of the four-sided die lands me a paltry 1. Boo! Then I roll a 3. Better. Finally, I roll another measly 1. Horrible! I multiply five (1+3+1=5) by ten and come up with fifty. That's twenty-five gp short of the sorcerer average. So far this little game of fantasy is feeling very realistic.

"That sucks," I tell Teddy, hoping he has some Dungeon Master trust fund spell he can cast on me. "I can barely afford socks, let alone my dream shoes."

"Don't worry. You'll be fine," Teddy says. "Sorcerers don't use a lot of weapons. You'll be relying on spells cast from memory and your Charisma."

Great, I think. I'm playing the elf version of Oliver Twist. *Please sir, can I have some more gold pieces? I saw the most darling little jacket and I'm out of conditioner.*

Does This Chainmail Make Me Look Fat?

Combat gear, like a Chanel suit and pair of Manolo sling backs, never goes out of style. And when you're set loose into a war zone, whether it's a first date, second interview, or third-level troll hell-bent on revenge, looking good is half the battle. Below are the standard armor and weapon choices for some of the most popular classes. And remember, if you can't run in heels, better pack a pair of cross-trainers.

Fighters and Rangers

Weapons: These bad boys and girls have their pick of the litter when it comes to weapons because they're highly skilled with almost all of them. Try a battleaxe or longsword for the greatest potential damage.

Armor: If it's not 1984 and you don't play guitar in a glam-rock band, it's hard to look good in studded leather, but somehow a ranger can pull it off. Fighters are better protected in the heaviest armor they can afford.

ARMOR ALL, ARMOR SOME

It's really no matter that I lack the funds to fill my designer backpack with weaponry. Sorcerers cannot use most weapons and instead rely on their spellcasting abilities. Personally, I think this is an advantage as I imagine my fellow adventurers, knees bent in proper form, heavy non-ergonomic backpacks, breastplates, and sheath-covered swords strapped onto their backs. They remind me of the mothers traveling solo on airplanes that hold everyone up when boarding because they've got seven Batman carry-ons, three strollers, twelve binkies, forty blankies, and seventeen thousand Baggies full of Cheerios. Me with my Chapstick, iPod, and copy of *Marie Claire* pity these women. And who wants to wear armor? Not flattering. Until Betsy Johnson designs a line of classic chainmail suits, I think I'll stick to my showgirl attire.

Ick. This armor is so last season.

Rogues

Weapons: The rogue's best weapon is his or her ability to sneak up on an opponent. Rapiers, daggers, and shortbows all lend to the art of surprise.

Armor: Rogues aren't quite as flashy as rangers and prefer the advantages of simple, timeless, unadorned leather armor.

Sorcerers and Wizards

Weapons: Their weapon choices are limited, so no excess baggage is needed. No matter, a sorcerer or wizard's best asset is his or her spellcasting ability anyway. And a winning smile, of course. For those rare occasions personality can't get you out of a big, fat mess, pick up a light crossbow.

Armor: Does this half-plate armor make my butt look big? Probably, so it's a good thing sorcerers and wizards don't wear armor. It interferes with their spellcasting ability and keen fashion sense.

Clerics

Weapons: Newbie clerics are only skilled in simple weapons, and that can be problematic for the holy man or woman who doesn't like being second best. A heavy mace and a shield offer the best protection. Like sorcerers, this class's biggest advantage comes from its magical abilities.

Armor: Straight up, a chain shirt is the best bet for optimal protection. The only downfall? What to match on the bottom.

Weapon of Choice

Backpacks? Food rations? Torches and lanterns? Sounds very much like we're spending a weekend at Yellowstone rather than vampire hunting in a fictional version of the Middle Ages. Sadly, I know people could just pull this stuff out of their closets along with a Triple-A TripTik® highlighting every dirt bed near a stream from their front door to the Grand Canyon. Me? I'm not one of those people. Roughing it means low thread-count sheets. And food rations? Now, there are two words that should never go hand in hand. My stomach begins to eat itself based on the prospect of living off of toothpaste and Velamints while shivering in my sleeping bag with a giant tree root jammed into my ribcage. Maybe I should consider reallocating my fantasy funds and invest in an air mattress and gastric bypass surgery.

Outfitting Astrid brings up a flood of empathy for my mother, who had to endure fourteen years of school shopping with me. And yes, fourteen—some of my greatest moments of fashion brilliance happened in pre-school. (Smock dresses over corduroy? Yep, been there, done that.) I would never have been happy with a standard package. One pair of two-toned jeans, two slouchy sweaters, and three pairs of leggings? I can't expect Astrid to settle either. Maybe I'll ask my friend at Parson's to whip up a chic yet environmentally appropriate outfit for an adventure-loving woman in her 130's. Some cargo pants and a fleece hoodie, perhaps?

Just like in real life, it's up to you to keep track of how much you're spending. Teddy doesn't dole out overdraft charges, but if you dream of beating down demons with a two-bladed sword and all you can afford is a butter knife, you'll need it because you'll be toast.

The starter package feels like the equivalent of sitting on a bench outside of JC Penney with the elderly husbands waiting for their wives to finish shopping, which may be why no one in my group chooses it. Or maybe scouring the racks of armor and finding that perfect scale mail overlay in your size, on sale, just like you saw in the magazines, has the same thrill for everyone. When all the characters have generated their random gold packages, Teddy sets us loose at Fashion Valley Mall.

"Excuse me," I ask Teddy, fantasy fondling the fantasy goods. "Is this backpack real leather?"

"Sure."

"Is it Balenciaga?"

"I don't know what you're asking me," Teddy says, pulling out the handbook. He doesn't like to send us anywhere, even REI for Rogues, unprepared.

"Ooh, get the matching wallet!" Lucy says, clapping her hands the way I imagine her baby might when she spies a Teletubbie.

"There's a clutch too," I point out. "Maybe I should get that? You know, for nighttime adventuring?"

Teddy nods his head. "You do need a component pouch in order to cast most of your spells, so go for it."

I don't correct Teddy and his blatant disregard for accessories. Pouches bring up visions of fanny packs, and Astrid is not a vendor at the ballpark or a fifty-something state fair-goer. Instead, I write down Balenciaga clutch under "Possessions" on my character sheet. I underline it lest there be any confusion.

"You're lucky you don't need to carry a lot of weaponry," Lucy says, wistfully. By the time this over, Ursula will be bogged down with 150 pounds of gear.

I glance at Astrid on the play mat, presumably perusing the sale racks. "On the contrary," I say, pointing out her miniscule red-tomato painted lips. "That lip color, it is definitely a weapon."

With my new designer carryall in hand, I leave the group to their armor fittings.

"I'll be at Jimmy Choo," I announce. "I'll meet you by Barnes and Noble."

Apparently Balenciaga stretches Teddy's imagination to its furthest capacity. "There is no Barnes and Noble. It's the Middle Ages."

"And there's no Jimmy Choo at Fashion Valley," Calvin says. "Which is too bad, really. You'll have to go to Nordstrom."

Helena throws down her pencil and shapeshifts from a thirty-year old Brand Manager to a three-year-old spoilsport. "Are we playing D&D or how to be a Hilton sister?"

"It's fantasy," Lucy says, coming to my aid. I bet she wishes Ursula would ditch the crap-kickers secured to her mighty calves and come shoe shopping with me.

"If Astrid wants to go shopping, let her," Armando pipes in. "She doesn't need to buy any weapons so there's no point in her just hanging around watching us." Armando is a sweet man who has all the makings of being a terrific husband someday.

"She could spend her money on a light source or food rations or any number of things that could help the whole group," Helena says. I'm four feet away from her, but she chooses to take up my selfish spending with Armando instead of me. Maybe she thinks I really do know how to cast some spells. *Duct tape to the mouth*, perhaps?

"No problem," I say. "I'll stop at Costco and pick up a few forty-pound bags of trail mix. Meet me there instead."

"Make sure you get the kind with M&Ms in it," Hank says. Before Helena can call metagaming on him he adds, "Yakama needs to keep his sugar levels up."

"Fine," Teddy says, "Everyone meet Astrid outside of Costco." Then to me, "You really should consider getting a weapon. At first level, you only know a handful of spells and they will run out quickly."

I get what he's saying. As a 1st-level sorcerer, I can only cast five 0-level spells and three 1st-level spells a day (more on that later). I don't want to be a drain on my team and will do no good cowering in the corner every time a moth flies by, no matter how well coordinated my accessories are.

"Have you seen the heel on a these shoes?" I ask. "I could most definitely inflict some damage with these bad boys."

"I hope you can run in them," Calvin says, and I picture Amok chasing Astrid through the high-backed cherry wood booths at our local pub. He gets an imaginary high-heeled kick to the shins and Astrid gets a crossbow.

Lotions and Potions and Plasma Screen TVs

You know those friends who have all the latest in techie gear and know how to use it? They've turned their living rooms into miniature Cineplexes with coffee tables and shag rugs. They've never missed an episode of *CSI* no matter what locale (which to me is magical all in itself). The acquisition of such goods in real life is equivalent to the magic items one can unearth in D&D. By now you might be thinking I'm droning on and on about my character's coolness factor, and even to me I sound like the annoying parent of a prospective pageant rat who tapes her kid's headshot to the vending machine and holds you hostage in the elevator while Little Miss Junior Pea Patch sings her sparkling rendition of "I Will Always Love You." Thus, another good reason to take the stairs. But really, whether you play a fighter or a rogue or any number of other characters who rely on good old-fashioned crossbows and left hooks, having magical gear in your adventuring group will benefit you too.

What are these magic items I speak of? They come in the form of potions and wands and rods and staffs, and magical armor, scrolls, weapons, and rings. (Anyone else got "Rudolph the Red Nosed Reindeer" in their head?)

I'm not talking about all those little jars crammed into your medicine cabinet. D&D potions are even more powerful than glycolic and salicylic acid combined. They're one-time-only drinks that give your character short-term effects like heightened strength or invisibility, kind of like a shot of Jagermeister.

Rings conjure up all sorts of stereotypes. You might be thinking about hobbits, remote locations, and exceptional cinematography, or you might be fantasizing about "the one ring to rule them all"—a Tiffany's princess cut platinum engagement ring. Regardless, you and your party will probably become betrothed to a few on your travels that offer various levels of protection and tax breaks.

We all know how important accessorizing is, and what is a magical maven without her magic wand? We're not talking the kind some kiddie magician bonks you on the head with to conjure a fabulous array of multicolor polyester scarves. We're talking wands that hold a single spell with multiple uses. It's like bulk spellcasting. You can find these magic wands next to the six-pack of memory foam mattresses and seventy-ounce cans of tuna. Astrid purchased a *wand of magic missile* that not only looked good with her Balenciaga clutch purse, it housed fifty of her favorite *magic missile* spells. No worries about maxing that one out in a day.

Rods are a tad high maintenance. They don't involve spells as much as powers. The cool thing is you can also use a rod as a weapon and whack an opponent (or a fellow adventurer who keeps asking for your phone number) over the head with it.

You might not think there is anything special about swords. I mean, what self-respecting swashbuckler doesn't have one these days? But these aren't your everyday run-of-the-mill swords. Occasionally, you and your group will come across a sword with a mind of its own. My group acquired a pile of loot left behind from an opponent we defeated. Part of his magical booty contained a sword with a major chip on its shoulder. When Jak went to claim it, he could feel the negative energy pour out of it. *Get yer filthy mitts off me,* it seemed to be saying. He quickly passed it on Ursula, who experienced the same reaction so she too passed it on. It's one thing to have a personified, love-struck candlestick or a motherly teapot, but a pissed off deadly weapon deserves a little coddling. Turns out the only person the sword would acquiesce to (and grudgingly, I might add) was Astrid. The sword was made by elves (my people) and it longed to be back with its own kind. I carried the sword the way some might carry a slobbery tennis ball to a black lab, with the little ingrate giving me the silent treatment the whole way back to town. We returned the prized possession to the elven embassy, and in kind we were treated to a fat reward. I wasted no time spending my share on what is by far my coolest possession—a *wand of mage hand.*

Ever been so comfortable on the couch that you couldn't fathom getting up for the remote control a mere six feet away, so you surrendered to nine hours of infomercials? Sure, you're now the proud owner of six cases of a citrus-smelling cleaner that promises to eat the concrete off the foundation, and the amazing egg cooker that guarantees perfectly boiled eggs in half the time it takes to toast a slice of bread, but you could have been watching something with a little more relevance—like a documentary of the excavation of an Egyptian tomb or an *America's Next Top Model* marathon. But now there's *mage hand!* The 0-level spell that allows you to magically lift and move any unattended object weighing less than five pounds! That's five unattended pounds of magical, moving material goods at your mercy! But wait—that's not all! You can move this object as far as fifteen feet! Impress your friends with your ability to pilfer invitations to an exclusive party. Swipe an ancient missing scroll from a defeated umber hulk's loot without getting your hands dirty! *Mage hand* does it all! If you order now we'll throw in this spell pouch fanny pack absolutely free! Don't miss out!

I used *mage hand* to snag us invitations to a masquerade ball. Once inside, I used *mage hand* to lift a handful of extra maraschino cherries into my red-hot mama. Apparently Astrid, like her mommy, can't handle her tequila. More on that later.

Uh Oh, It's Magic

Every class has its advantages. Forget pulling a quarter from behind your ear—rogues have way cooler tricks up their sleeves. They are highly skilled in the small weapons field and often hit their mark before the poor schlub even heard the shrill of the shot. Picture Inspector Gadget with biceps. Barbarians get to rage against the monster and are almost always going to kick some serious butt. Think The Rock or Vin Diesel or any female wrestler who has the ability to hang you on the wall like a Monet with one mega paw around your neck, screaming "You want a piece of this?"

Call me biased, but I can't help admiring the subtler combatant. The one who has the ability to intimidate from afar, whether hiding behind the boulder or locked in the women's bathroom. That's right—the magic men and women of D&D. Several classes have the ability to cast spells, but before you decide which spells you want to cast, you'll need to decide which type of spellcaster you want to play. It's not just wizards and sorcerers who can cast spells. If magic is your game you can also play a bard, druid, or a cleric. Day after day, these characters engage in the ultimate spelling bee. Some whiz kid from the plains of South Dakota might be able to spell *telekinesis* without spell check (and for the record, I can't, but I'm not from South Dakota), but can she bull rush the class bully from the lunch room to the locker room with the blink of an eye? Didn't think so. But hey, kid, cool trophy.

Sorry, Lucky—your pink hearts and yellow moons have nothing on Astrid's arsenal of charms. What spells, you ask? How about the ability to cast a *magic missile* that always hits its mark (even from the bathroom stall) or *detect magic,* which can pinpoint magical auras. Or how about *acid splash,* which allows you to douse your opponent with a burning orb of acid. Yep, it's the stuff *Lifetime Television for Women* movies are made of. A sorcerer can pretty much do that one in her sleep.

Think of 0-level spells as a gift-with-purchase. They're the equivalent of the starter set that came with your favorite toy. You got just enough pieces to learn how to play and whet your appetite for more. 0-level spells may not be the most glamorous or wield the most power, but they're free for the taking. And you even get to choose which spells you want, so you'll never be stuck with a tiny tube of lip gloss that completely washes you out.

Spells have levels just like characters do. The higher your level, the cooler, more powerful spells you can learn. It's kind of like elementary school. First grade taught you how to count by twos while percentages eluded you until fifth grade. I don't like math, but I do like being able to figure out what an additional 40% off the winter coat I've been eyeing adds up to.

The hardest part about spellcasting is deciding which spells you want. Sorcerers and bards can cast spells from memory, meaning once a spell is checked off the long list on your character sheet, you can cast it at any time—no chemistry set needed. However, they can't customize their spell list daily to prepare for the challenges at hand. For instance, if you knew you were heading into vampire territory the next day, you'd probably want to prepare a spell like *disrupt undead* before bed. Should a sorcerer or a bard encounter a band of batmen, she'd better hope *disrupt undead* is a spell already on her list. Also, these classes are given a maximum allotment of spells to cast per day. A 1st-level sorcerer, for instance, can only cast five 0-level spells and three 1st-level spells when starting out. A high score in Charisma could net a few more, and she'll pocket more spells as she gains experience.

Sound confusing? It's like this: Say you come to work with five M&Ms and three Twix bars everyday. You might want an M&M with your morning coffee and a Twix bar after your lunch to counteract the Cobb salad taste lingering on your buds. Perhaps later in the day, a co-worker the next cube over is talking very loudly on his cell phone to his doctor about chronic digestive issues. You realize throwing a stapler might lead to assault charges so you zing an M&M at his unprotected ear. Make it a peanut one so it stings more, but not so much he won't feel embarrassed telling HR he was knocked unconscious by a piece of candy. Now you're left with only three M&Ms and two Twix bars. Use them wisely—you still have a staff meeting, your mid-year review, and a long, congested commute home. When you've eaten the last of your candy, it's all gone and you might as well go to bed. You'll wake up to a fresh new supply.

Now, if you're the kind of person who can limit yourself to only five M&Ms per day, then congratulations—you're a freak of nature and clearly have more power than any menacing monster D&D can muster. If you're a mere mortal like the rest of us and can't wait to add more delicious chocolates to your cache, you can do so only after leveling up.

If you're of the other spell throwing variety like a cleric or wizard, you can customize your spell list each day. As opposed to a sorcerer who casts the spells she knows from memory, a wizard or cleric can only cast spells he's prepared in advance, so choose wisely. So if you, say, had a big presentation due at work, instead of organizing your index cards the night before, you could summon Joan Rivers. That way, you'd be at ease on the podium, explaining in your charming self-depreciating way why this year's numbers are forecasted below projections before explaining to the CEO that the hemline on her skirt makes her calves look like they should be holding up a baby grand piano. The next day you could incorporate *update resume* into your spell list and summon Sally Struthers, who can help you foster your dream of becoming a vet technician with a flair for interior design.

Spelling Under the Influence

Spells are powerful tools, my friends, and can take less concentration to cast than a second-grade production of *Little Red Riding Hood*. That being said, watch where you're pointing that finger and be extra sure you mean what you say. Especially if you're not in combat and have, say, the overwhelming taste of maraschino cherries in your mouth.

I've embraced the fact that my character's biceps will never look like Angela Bassett's in *What's Love Got to Do With It?* And she'll probably never be picked first for kickball. I have not, however, embraced the fact that my character could bite it in battle and I'd be forced to do all that math again. (Or rather, watch Teddy do it all again.) In the same vein as a supermodel who insures her calves for millions of dollars, there are some precautions a sorcerer can take to help protect her assets as well.

A 0-level spell may not seem like much, but it's enough for a sorcerer to learn *detect magic*. Think you're the only one who can cast a dangerous spell? Think again. With this spell, you'll be able to sniff out evil from sixty feet away.

Daze is another good 0-level spell. It's not your dazzling good looks and winning smile this time. It's a spell meant to stun a humanoid creature into losing its next turn.

Learn how to cast *mage armor*, a 1st-level spell, as soon as possible. *Mage armor* surrounds the creature of your choice (and yep, the creature can be you) with an invisible force field, increasing your Armor Class by 4 points. And let's face it—a force field is a lot more flattering than a breastplate.

Any sorcerer worth her wand will tell you that *magic missile* saves more butts than stretch denim and a good G-string put together. It's a 1st-level spell, so you won't go too long without it.

Two more good spells for the physically challenged are the 2nd-level spells, *resist energy* and *mirror image*. *Resist energy* keeps bad juju in the form of acid, cold, electricity, fire, or sonic energy at bay. *Resist energy* is hard to resist, especially in real life where it would come in handy. Kind of an "I'm rubber—you're glue" scenario. There's safety in numbers, and *mirror image* creates several illusionary duplicates of yourself, making it difficult for your opponent—and your party—to determine which one is the real deal.

When you get 3rd-level spells? Forget it. There are too many good ones to choose from. *Fireball, lightning bolt, haste* . . . you get the picture. And it only gets better.

Mirror Image

Yŏu Cast a Spell ŏn Me

Friends shouldn't let friends cast spells on themselves unless it's absolutely necessary. Especially if you have a limited number of spells per day, and it's unlikely you'll get jumped by a band of wild trolls before you can unroll your sleeping bag. Fortunately, it's not all about camping and roughing it. I was surprised and delighted to find so many pubs populating these imaginary worlds, and our characters often need to unwind after a long day of adventuring. Tasked with tracking an evasive opponent, Astrid and friends retreated to a local watering hole to review their game plan. We hadn't found our elusive opponent, but we did encounter happy hour. It was a long night, what can I say? When the real me left the room to refill my water and M&M supply, the mini me was dancing on tables when I returned.

"What the heck is going on?" I asked, looking at Astrid standing on the circle marked "*table*" in blue marker.

"Astrid couldn't resist," Calvin said. "She saw a table and some men in suits, and it made her miss her day job."

I shot Lucy a "how could you let this happen?" look, but she was too busy blotting the tears of laughter running down her face to notice. Ursula is a sucky wingman.

Once Astrid was back on solid ground, an official-looking stranger in uniform approached her. Who was this man? What did he want with her? Why did he choose to speak with her rather than her friends? Did he really think she was a stripper? Perhaps it was the six pints of mead or maybe it was Astrid's skittish personality: She panicked and cast *resist energy* on herself, believing the man was going to pull some funny business. He wasn't. He just needed directions. Astrid spent the last of her spells and the rest of the night stumbling around in her protective bubble. Unfortunately, *resist energy* doesn't protect against the mocking of your peers.

How to Spell Pizzazz

Sure, it's enough for some people to view a D&D adventure the same as they would the Sunday crossword puzzle. It's something to solve, a clever and challenging way to wile away your day. Others are more apt to view D&D as a portal out of your mundane human self and into the life of a parallel you who doesn't just know how to bludgeon every bone in a skeleton's undead body, but who relishes the opportunity to do so. The real me doesn't even like watching people eat chicken wings.

Here's where some of the stereotypes might come into play again, like you *have* to dress like your character or learn to speak in an affected British

TOP 10 SPELLS EVERY WOMAN SHOULD KNOW

It's an unpredictable world out there, but with knowledge of the following enchantments, you can finally spell relief.

✳ **Teleport (5th level):** The best time to leave a party is while it's still in full swing. Good times can turn to bad times in no time and this spell will get you and your pals out of there quicker than a bat out of where the party was soon heading.

✳ **Charm Person (1st level):** Never read another boring book with "How," "To," "Influence," "Successful," "Cheese," or "Habits" in the title. With charm person under your belt you'll be making friends with a simple point of the finger.

✳ **Resist Energy (2nd level):** Sticks and stones can break your bones but bad energy can't touch you.

✳ **Find the Path (6th level):** Never take the scenic route by accident again. With this spell, you'll literally have a built-in satellite system at your fingertips.

✳ **Ventriloquism (1st level):** Who said that? Dunno. With the ability to throw your voice from pretty much anywhere, it was probably you. Great spell for those pugnacious types whose mouths are often greater than their muscles. And it's a great party trick, too.

✳ **Break Enchantment (4th or 5th level depending on which class you play):** What the heck does your best pal see in that cheating, disrespectful low-life? She won't see it for long. This spell frees victims from curses, spells, enchantments, and dead-end relationships.

✳ **Calm Emotions (2nd level):** If you need to use break enchantment, you've probably pulled this one out too. Use it to soothe a disconcerted creature. It's a gooey brownie sundae for the soul.

✳ **Sleet Storm (3rd level):** So what if it's the middle of May? Some days we all need a little extra sleep. When you choose to snooze, conjure a freak storm from the comfort of your comforter.

✳ **Glitterdust (2nd level):** They can run, but they can't hide. Drop the glitter bomb anytime, anywhere, and not only do you have an instant party, you've blinded your opponents and revealed invisible predators.

✳ **Invisibility (2nd level)** and **Fly (3rd level):** Technically these are numbers 10 and 11, but they're both kind of a no-brainers and way too cool to choose between. Who wouldn't love to engage in a little out-of-sight adventure every now and then? Especially from sixty feet in the air.

highbrow accent. Not true. But it doesn't hurt, or shockingly, embarrass you to maybe get into character a little bit.

When I imagine a sorcerer's closet, all I can picture is Susannah the Pet Psychic who I met at a summer street fair. She offered to do a reading on my then fourteen-year-old Alaskan malamute. She wore a long patchwork skirt, brown leather sandals, a sheer white blouse, and multicolored scarves around her naturally frizzed-out hair. Although I couldn't spot them, I know something on her had bells because I heard a ding-a-ling-a-ling every time she raised her arms to do a chakra check. Come to think of it, the ding-a-ling-a-ling could have been the sound of my common sense leaving the building. I think I'll stick to jeans and T-shirts, thanks very much.

It's just not enough to say, "I want to cast a *magic missile* spell, please." Not when you're playing a game where imagination is essential and fantasy is key. How would one cast a *magic missile*? Where would it shoot from and what would it sound like when it launched? Obviously you'd need to be standing to launch a missile, right? I pictured magic skyrockets in flight firing from my wrists. Talk about afternoon delight! Instead of telling the gaming group what Astrid was about to do, it seemed very natural to show them. I stood up, flipped my hands back, and shouted in a high-pitched voice that could make dolphins weep: "Puem puem!"

The first time I did it, I got strange looks from the group.

"What was that?" Hank asked.

"Are you okay?" Armando asked.

"Uh . . . bless you?" Calvin (as Amok) said.

"Are you trying to cast a spell?" Helena asked. "Or are you channeling Spider-Man?

Spider-Man! Curses! I thought the wrist thing was original.

"I get it!" Lucy called out. "It's a *magic missile*."

If I had a hundred dollars or a new washer and dryer, I'd give it to her for correctly identifying my actions.

"Okay, then," Teddy said. "Astrid just cast *magic missile*. Roll for damage, Astrid."

Helena cringed. "We don't all have to that, right?" she asked. "Make those little sounds?" She might as well have been complaining about having to pick off her fingernails with a pair of pliers judging by the face she made. *Do I have to?*

"You can't cast a magic missile, Monky Brewster," I reminded her. "Your little fists of fury don't have . . . *the magic*." I did some variation of jazz hands when I said "magic." I'm glad I didn't have a mirror to see myself.

"You're a shifter," Teddy told her. "You don't generally make noise."

If only, I thought.

Besides Helena, no one questioned me turning our group into a midnight showing of the *Rocky Horror Picture Show*. In fact, they began to look forward to Astrid leveling up so new effects, both magic and audible, would be added to our game. I've got *ray of enfeeblement* that goes "waawaawaawaawaawaah," and *ray of frost* that makes a "whooooosh" sound when I point my index finger at the offender. *Acid splash* involves both hands above my head as if I'm throwing a giant beach ball. It makes a *splat* upon contact. Sound effects have become a regular part of our game. Ursula's greatsword makes a *whap whap* in combat. Jak insists on a "booya" when his rapier makes contact with a beast. Amok thinks it's appropriate to sing *Hail to the Chief* when he busts out the healing spells. We're not so amenable to that one.

Whatever enhancements you bring to your game, you can guarantee one sound effect—laughter. And who cares if you embarrass yourself? What happens in a D&D adventure stays with the adventure unless one of you happens to be writing a book.

Dear Diary,

Had a fun day of S&S—shopping and spelling. Needed to get some gear, so Ursula and I headed off to Fashion Valley Mall. Picked up the cutest spell pouch. Well, okay, pouches, but everyone knows how quickly you can go through them in an adventure. That's another reason I figured it was acceptable to drop a hefty amount of coin on baggage. I have none! And I'm not just talking the hobo and clutch variety. Poor Ursula had a hard time finding scale armor. Yuck. That stuff is so unflattering and it's almost impossible to find scale mail leggings in her size. Nobody makes a decent pair with a twenty-two inch inseam. I gave her the name of my seamstress. She's done some pretty magical things with a swatch of fabric. Unfortunately, we ran into Miss Shifty Shifter Tenoctris in the parking lot. Is this girl always in trouble or what? I wish she'd shift herself into a breeze and blow out of here. Instead she asked us, or rather Ursula, to meet her later at the Red Dragon.

"Bring Amok and Yakama," she said, before making a point of looking right me and saying, "And Jak."

You know what's worse than a pissed-off, intolerant sorcerer with impulsive tendencies? A best friend who can read you like a scroll. Ursula put a firm hand on mine and told the little monkey wench that she makes it a point to never go adventuring without a wickedly talented, not to mention impeccably accessorized, sorcerer. I think Ursula knew Tenoctris was three seconds shy of an acid splash facial, but seeing as though I can only blast off five a day, she was right to rein me in. Knowing if she wanted Ursula's company I was the gift-with-purchase, all Tenoctris could say to me was "Wear comfortable shoes."

"I like your shoes," Ursula said after Mighty Mouth finally left. "You'll be fine."

I decided to treat Ursula to a pedicure. But first, I think I'll work on some new spells. I don't trust Tenoctris as far as I can throw her, which isn't really that far at all.

More later.

Love, Astrid

TOP 10 REASONS
D&D IS BETTER THAN DATING

1. Getting dumped only costs a few hit points.

2. Hitting on someone usually involves a *magic missile* or a mace.

3. *Protection from evil* spells—need I say more?

4. Your wingman knows forty-two spells and is proficient with a longsword.

5. "Being experienced" is something to brag about.

6. Traveling in packs with your girlfriends doesn't involve wearing pink tulle headgear and charging strangers a buck to suck Lifesavers off your shirt.

7. First dates often consist of meeting bugbears and dire wolves—not ex-wives and parents.

8. Failed relationships can be blamed on bad die rolls.

9. Character sheets give you the ability to check out a guy's stats before a first date.

10. If you get hurt, chances are you'll be healed by morning.

Protection from Evil: When you care enough to protect the very best.

Chapter Four
LOVE IS A BATTLEFIELD

Fantasy life isn't just shopping and spellcasting, and some of us are still coming to terms with that. Into every life a little conflict must fall, and truer words were never spoken in the world of D&D. It's about adventure, right? While some of us might view an outlet mall as an adventure and trying to find your size amid the endless racks a contact sport, D&D engages its players in battles of the mind and body. You've spent all this time preparing for it, Grasshopper. Now is your time to shine.

Some would say the essence of a DUNGEONS & DRAGONS game is the rock 'em sock 'em part. Others would say the heart of the game lies in the storytelling. Almost every guy who has had women step up to the table will tell you the game becomes less about slashing the throat of any old troll who happens to look sideways at you and more about finding out *why* he's looking at you. Women, the male gamers say, are also more into enhancing their skill sets than building their biceps and gravitate toward the healing-and-nurturing classes, like clerics.

It's a plausible theory, but one that's completely debunked as I look around my gaming table. Little Lucy is practicing her signature growls, "Arr" and "Urg" and "Ursula wants to get drunk and fight." Helena is cracking her knuckles like a street fighter trying to unlock the fists of fury. She stares intently at the play mat, daring a predator to cross our paths. None of these women, myself included, are the type to jump out from behind a Volkswagen and sucker punch someone in the parking lot (Helena is much more the type to tell HR that you steal Post-Its and microwave popcorn), but Monday afternoons we check the animal lover, new mom, and office narc at the door. Sure, I feel protective of Astrid out there alone on the play mat. I picture her running through the door after combat screaming, "Mommy, Mommy! I beat an old dusk hag with a *flaming sphere*. You would have been so proud!" And yes, before any potential run-in, I pretend she's three seconds from claiming she forgot about a dentist appointment and the only thing she'll be beating is out of there. But here's my dirty little secret: I like the shoot 'em up part of the game too. I love when my character casts *magic missiles* and fires her crossbow. I know I've developed a character who, with the help of her friends, can match wits with almost any opponent the Dungeon Master throws our way. I like the element of surprise, not knowing when a band of angry goblins will jump in our path or what grudge-holding creature we'll accidentally unearth on our quest

Battle grid

to find a missing scroll. I like this side of me almost as much as knowing I *have* this side of me.

And when it's over, Astrid, my pencils, my Ziploc bag full of borrowed dice, and my broken-in copy of the *Player's Handbook* go back in the black tote bag I bought especially for this purpose and I go back to my desk, type a few emails, think about dinner, call my mom, and go home. Unlike most of the working world, I love Mondays.

On this particular Monday, Teddy is busy setting up shop. He puts up a cardboard screen so we can't see what sinister foils he's plotting. It's here where the zombies and flesh-eating golems await their chance to knock us off our path. It's where the story unfolds, backstage or behind the magical curtain. I still don't know exactly what he does back there. I do know that D&D is a lot easier to imagine if you can visually see where you are, which is why we use miniatures and a battle grid, or play mat. Teddy uses a wet-erase marker to draw the playing field on the battle grid. Each one-inch square on the grid equals five feet. This is how we determine how far our characters are moving or, in Astrid's case, how far she is from serious trouble.

A D&D adventure can take on many shapes. A *roleplaying encounter* is one in which your character interacts with any character the Dungeon Master controls. An example would be trying to sell a used spiked metal shield ransacked from a slain opponent to a band of goblins. Tough sell, believe me. Trying to navigate your way through a rat-infested sewer system while trying to protect the missing piece of a long-sought-after scroll in your rucksack is considered a *challenge encounter*. Probably the most conventional encounter, and what some consider the core of the game, is the *combat encounter*. Here is where your character goes head to horned head with some of the game's most dreaded beasts.

Basic Training

No soldier worth her boot straps would go to battle without learning the rules of engagement. DUNGEONS & DRAGONS may sound like a big bucket of bedlam, but there is a method to the madness. Heed another one of Mr. Rogers' rules—wait your turn—and you, like many of these rules, will be golden.

Does "roll for initiative" sound familiar? It will. You might remember it's how to determine who goes first in combat. Check your character sheet (or Astrid's in Chapter 6 until you create your own) and you'll notice the *initiative modifier*. This is the number you'll add to your twenty-sided die roll. The character with the highest number (or initiative) goes first, second highest goes second, and so on. A round ends when everyone has taken a turn. When you roll for initiative, the Dungeon Master rolls for your opponent so there's always a chance a ghoul jumps out from behind a tree, puts you in a headlock, and lands a right hook to your nose before you've even unsheathed your weapon.

So when it is your turn, you're not just going to stand there, right? At the very least you'll cover your vitals and drop down in the fetal position. More likely your character will do one of the following things:

Move and attack: Maybe it's you who jumps out from a tree and sucker punches a ghoul. You'll need to be in fist throwing distance to do this, so you'll move your miniature across the battle grid and let it fly.

Attack and move: By far my favorite maneuver. Hit 'em with your best shot and run away.

Move only: Gelatinous cubes have no respect for personal space. Sometimes your best option is to just back away. Slowly. Sometimes you'll move in one round to get into perfect position to pounce in the next round.

Attack only: One of the coolest things about *magic missiles* is that they always hit their target. Even from far, far away, so there's no reason to duck and cover. You're probably already doing that.

If making a move were a group effort in real life, there would be a lot fewer people staying home alone on Friday nights. Alas, it's not in the real world, but that kind of cooperation is as common as tiramisu at an Italian restaurant in the D&D world. Here's where the team aspect really comes into play: taking turns, showing off your various skills, protecting one another, and slipping in a quick healing when someone gets hurt. Say we encounter a zombie with 20 hit points. Ursula puts the smack down on him with her greatsword and deals 10 points of damage. Jak gets in a good whap with his rapier for 5 points. Then Astrid casts off a few *magic missiles* and dings the creature for 6 points. What do you get? A dead undead who's been hit with more damage than his hit points could withstand.

We take great pride in taking down our opponents. Teddy knocks over the mini representing the bad guy before removing it from the play mat and we erupt into cheers. I half expect to look around the table and see painted faces and someone starting the wave.

ROLL WITH IT

As you probably know by now, dice play an essential role in the game of *Dungeons & Dragons*. Players roll the dice to determine the fate of their characters. The DM rolls for the opponent. Commit the core game mechanic to memory: Any time your character attempts an action that involves the chance of not succeeding, roll your twenty-sided die, add the appropriate modifier, and hope for a big number. If you hit, you roll the appropriate die to see how much damage you inflict. You can take the following kinds of actions.

Attack rolls: Does the bolt you fired from your crossbow hit its target?

Skill checks: There's a rustling in the shrubs behind the abandoned shack. Do you hear it?

Ability checks: You attempt to get all Jet Li on a secret door. Break it down or break a toe?

Ah, if only all of life's decisions were made by the roll of a die.

Hit Me with Your Best Shot

It's true that atypical weapons can do the most damage. I once went on a date with a man who almost bored me to death with his vapid personality. Do you know the symptoms of a chinch-bug infested plant? I do, and I'm not afraid to use this information should you invade my personal space. And once I had to perform the Heimlich on four members of a holiday cookie swap after they tasted my homemade sugar cookies. Or rather, salt cookies. Oh, come on! They're both white and grainy. Who hasn't dumped a little salt on their corn flakes at least once? When dull dates and recipe malfunctions are not at your disposal, your character will probably inflict damage with a more typical weapon like a sword or a longbow. Here's how to attack and calculate damage with your chosen weapon.

Look at the section of your character sheet where your weapons are housed. It will look something like this:

Attack	Attack Bonus	Damage
Shortspear	+1	1d6

1. Roll a twenty-sided die and add any modifiers like bonuses or penalties. (In this case, you'll add +1 to your total.)
2. If the total is equal to or greater than your opponent's Armor Class, you hit. (The Dungeon Master knows the opponent's Armor Class. You're on a need-to-know basis.)
3. If you hit, roll the appropriate die for that weapon and add any modifier. (In this case you would roll 1d6, or one six-sided die.) The number you roll is deducted from the opponent's hit points.
4. When the opponent's hit points are reduced to 0, consider it deader than a pop singer's acting career.

Doing Unto Others As They Can Do Unto You

Common sense dictates that if you can make the bad guys drop and give you twenty, they can do the same to you.

Remember your hit points (or HP) on your character sheet? That's how much damage your character can take. When an opponent has dropped your hit points to 0, your character's only move is a single move. That means you can roll your beaten carcass into a ditch to avoid further damage or maybe call your naturopath and ask for some emergency breathing exercises, but that's about it. But don't panic—yet. Here's where a negative is really a positive. You have all the way to −10 before your character actually dies. When your hit points reach −1 or fewer, your character makes like a

YO MUMMY

Astrid had a friend named Artemis who was punched in the face by a mummy and quickly reduced to a pile of dust. She died, and there was nothing anyone could do about it. The cause? Mummy rot. Don't laugh, it can happen to you too. Curing mummy rot takes serious magical mojo, but you can prevent it easily enough: Don't let a mummy touch you. Distance is your best defense.

This has been a Public Service Announcement brought to you by Rage Against Rot.

soap opera diva and falls ultra-glamorously into an unconscious stupor. Only you won't be wearing a clingy, red Dolce and Gabbana dress and full makeup. It is here, in this ditch while your teammates rage on, that those life-before-your-eyes flashbacks occur and you'll reunite with your kindergarten teacher who you now realize never really liked kids after all. She'll show you all the horrible stuff you did, above and beyond tattling and finger painting the class hamster.

Remember that time you convinced Richard to climb to the top of the jungle gym, knowing he'd never be able to make his way down?

Gasp! How did you know?

You pointed and laughed at him and told him he never should have listened to you.

You hope that your group can defeat the evil bastard that did this to you quickly because your character loses another hit point with each round of play. When your character's points have dropped to −10, it's pencils down. As in dead. As in biting the big one. Cashed out. Knock, knock, knocking on heaven's door. Sowing the Elysian Fields. Need a moment to reflect on this? Your character can die. I've heard stories about people who have played a character for years, only to have him or her snuffed out by a baby red dragon. I've heard tales of Dungeon Masters who have virtual graveyards for the PCs they've knocked off. My Astrid reduced to a pile of pencil shavings? Oh no you didn't!

See why it's so important to play nice with the cleric, even if he is a conceited pervert who thinks your character is an exotic dancer? Your holy friend has the power to undo damage with the roll of a die. If he chooses to heal you during combat, this counts as his action. All it takes is 1 or more hit points to get you back in the game.

I have to admit, the thought of losing Astrid to a swarm of dire rats freaks me out, and not just because I'm not sure Teddy would go through the trouble of building me another character. I *like* Astrid, her brassy hair and club girl wardrobe and growing list of spells nestled inside a designer spell pouch. I smile at the thought of a pre-pubescent elf sitting in her little pink bedroom, making the electricity go on and off while she tries to gain control of her new powers.

Astrid, knock it off until after Murder She Wrote, okay?

Astrid has family and friends and store credit cards. She has a personality and exquisite taste and her position on this team matters. I've invested hours into raising my elf princess. She must be protected!

Dungeon Tours Begin at 3:00

Contrary to what we just talked about, it's not always about kicking butt. Do you spend hours watching HGTV? Do you visit realtor's websites just to get a peek into homes you can't afford? Do you ever drop into an open house on your way to the bank? How many times have you actually been inside a monster-rich dungeon? Maybe you want to spend some quality time checking out the mysterious digs, kicking down doors, scouring for secret passages, and looting treasure. Almost any time Astrid enters a new locale, she scouts out magical auras by casting *detect magic*. In my mind it's equivalent to those handheld metal detectors little old men use on the beaches every morning in search of quarters and lost watches. *Beep. Beep. Beep, beep, beep, beep!* In the game world, it's a very practical spell. The world is your playground, or at least in this case your play mat, so have fun with it.

The Etiquette of War

I knew there'd be some skepticism about whether I would return for a second session. I suppose I don't outwardly embody the traits of a typical roleplayer (we killed those stereotypes already, right?), male or female—and if I do possess them, I'm hiding them better than a celeb's post-baby tummy tuck. My biggest doubter was Helena, who gets into character by shifting herself into a big, black cloud when I take my seat at the conference room table.

"Oh cool!" I say. "Are you taking Negotiating with Hostile Coworkers 101, or are you the example?"

"I thought you might have a conflict with your weekly manicure," she says, which is totally stupid. My weekly manicure is on Fridays.

"Hey everyone," Calvin shouts. "The stripper has arrived! You can set up over there in the corner."

"Leave her alone," Lucy says, pumping her fist in Calvin's direction. "Or Ursula will make you."

"Did you bring more rabbit food?" Hank asks, shoving a handful of salt and vinegar chips into his piehole.

I did bring my rabbit food and bottled water, along with a makeshift dice bag to house my hand-me-down dice.

"Is that lingerie on the table?" Armando asks, backing away.

I pick the item in question up with my index and pinky finger and wave it in his face. "Oh, crap. I brought my hand washing instead of my dice bag."

Armando yelps and turns such a frightening shade of red I thought mercury would come bursting through his pupils.

It wasn't lingerie, of course. *That* would be bad etiquette. It was the pouch my gift-with-purchase perfume sample came in that just happened to be black, lacy, and very dainty, yet roomy enough for a set of dice. Armando's dice are carried in a brown pleather pouch. Lucy uses a velvet satchel from a bottle of Crown Royal. Hank totes his dice in an Altoids tin.

Although we see each other all day, there's still so much to talk about. We cover weekend recaps, what's in our Netflix queue, tonight's episode of *24,* and how much hotter Kiefer Sutherland is now than he was in *Young Guns.* Teddy chooses to finish drawing the map rather than weigh in on Kiefer's hotness. He stands at the head of the table and waits for us to notice him.

"I've got two hours," he says. "It's up to you on what we do with them." He's a master at the "I'm not mad; I'm just disappointed" look. We apologize for acting disrespectful and focus our undivided attention on him.

Satisfied, Teddy doesn't waste anymore time getting us back into the adventure. He recaps where we left off. After our shopping spree at the city of Sharn's beautiful outdoor mall, Fashion Valley, we prance along the cobblestones en route from Ye Olde Mead and Ale Factory in all our spendthrift glory. We're adorned in our new duds—shining armor, weapons sheathed, we've got bellies full of Thai lettuce wraps and turtle cheesecake and we're ready for anything as long it follows a nap. Maybe we'll go to a movie later. What's bad about this day?

Need I ask? I forgot about that shadowy villain who vanished over the railing and is still a source of contention. This time we have a full two hours to figure out what to do about him.

"Remember," Teddy says. "Tenoctris and Yakama noticed the figure escaping and saw an unidentified clump on the cobblestones. What do you want to do?"

"Let's check it out," Helena as Tenoctris says, all brave and coy.

Oh, Tenoctris, you're my hero. She probably kills spiders and changes her own flat tires, too.

"Yakama is moving forward to see what the clump is," Hank tells us, and moves his miniature on the play mat.

"Fight! Fight!" Ursula says.

"Loot! Loot!" Jak says.

"Shop! Shop!" Astrid says. "I still have silver pieces."

"Scaredy cat," Amok says to Astrid, although it feels more like Calvin saying that to Shelly. Using the pretense of a D&D game to vet real life feelings is also bad etiquette.

"It's okay," Ursula says. "You can go shopping after we play. Now we kick ass."

That's true, but in real life I have a knock-off Prada with a broken zipper and a very tired debit card. What fun is that?

I'm outnumbered and that's fine. D&D is about majority ruling, and if you're smart, you'll go with it. A friend was just telling me how he bucked his party's advice, tumbled into a mystery cave, set off a lightning trap, and killed his entire group. No one wants to bear that burden. Besides, I have to admit I'm a little curious to see what these spells can do.

"A body lies on the floor of the bridge," Teddy tells us. "The rain mixes with a pool of blood around what appears to be the head."

I'm desperately trying to pay attention because the DM seldom gives you information that isn't relevant, but my ADD is surfacing again. I find myself thinking about what to make for dinner, how can I finagle a massage out of this month's budget, why Kiefer and Julia really broke up. . . .

". . . clutched tightly in the body's hand, surrounded by blood and gore."

"What's in his hand?" I ask, the blood and gore jarring me back to reality. I mean . . . fantasy.

"It's the new Fendi hobo bag," Calvin says. "The same one Beyoncé was seen wearing in St. Tropez."

"It's a leather satchel," Teddy says. "Not sure of the designer."

"It's covered in blood and gore," Lucy says. "Ew. You don't want that."

I find it rather odd that a woman who often wears regurgitated peas and breast milk on her lapel like it's a cherished heirloom brooch would find a little blood and innards disgusting.

"Is he dead?" Armando, as Jak, asks. He sounds sad, like when my brother asked my mom if the beta fish he left outside for the whole month of June was dead.

Teddy nods his head aggressively. "Oh yeah, he's definitely dead."

"Guts be damned," Yakama says, reaching for the satchel and rummaging through its contents. We find out the identity—an elderly provost from a university. We also come up ten silver pieces and two gold pieces richer.

Astrid and Tenoctris

Yakama hands the loot to Jak, who will be in charge of keeping track of what we have as a party and divvying up the goods. In addition to some quills, papers, and an apple, the satchel also contains the dead provost's journal. I suspect that will be important, but my priorities are elsewhere.

"So about this satchel. You said it was well made?"

"I'll give you the satchel," Armando says, writing it down.

"She already has a bag," Helena says.

A bag, I think. As in *one*? I'm starting to think Helena really is a shifter monk or something very far removed from female.

"My other bag is for daytime adventuring," I tell her. "I shall use this one for our evening romps." I tell her if we pilfer any fanny packs we'll give them straight to her. Using the pretense of a D&D game to vet—yeah, yeah, I know. . . .

Before she can counter, Teddy tells us the shadowy figure has returned and spots us.

"He's pissed off you stole his bag. Give it back, Astrid!" Amok shouts.

"Way to throw her under the bus," Hank tells his pal. "Here, Mr. Evil Shadow Stalker. Chew on this delightful elf while the rest of us get the hell out of here. She's magically delicious."

"He killed this guy and left the bag so it obviously wasn't a mugging," Astrid explains to Amok. "If he wanted the bag or its contents, he'd have had first dibs." Thankfully, Astrid didn't inherit my lack of control in a crisis. She stays calm, cool and collected. She's probably a Libra.

"The shadowy figure moves toward you," Teddy says, and we all make an "oooh" sound very similar to that of the studio audience on *Wheel of Fortune*. "You notice it's moving on four legs—not two!"

"A doggy!" I shout. "Come here, little puppywuppy." I volunteer at an animal shelter, so I have experience wrangling the canines. Maybe all this misunderstood beast needs is a good three-mile run.

"Are you crazy?" Jak yells. "Don't call that thing over here."

"Roll for initiative, everyone!" Teddy is getting excited. Is that sweat beading on his forehead?

Everyone does as they're told, except me who has suddenly forgotten what rolling for initiative means. I pick up my thirty-seven dice and yell, "Yahtzee!"

Lucy gently places the twenty-sided die in front of me. "Roll this one," she says in her nice mommy voice. "Add it to your initiative modifier."

Oh right. Combat. Oh no. Combat. Bad things really do happen in this game. Someone could get clubbed over the head or fall down a well or bitten in the neck or put to sleep. If I do something stupid or ill-advised like my lightning-trap friend did, my group could pay an awful price. What if I don't know enough spells? What if I don't know how to use them? What if my *magic missile* accidentally hits Tenoctris? Would that be so bad, really?

Rolling for initiative is how order is determined during combat. Just roll your twenty-sided die and add it to the initiative modifier on your character sheet.

I look around the table at the seventeens, fourteens, elevens, eights, and the patient eyes of my teammates as they wait for me to toss my twenty-sided die. I'm about to pray for a low number when I glance at Astrid's character sheet. The high Charisma and Dexterity. The small but carefully thought-out list of spells known. If Astrid did need to put her money where her mouth is, she'd be able to back it up. I roll a ten and add my paltry initiative modifier of 3—just enough to keep me firmly entrenched in the middle of the line.

Before it's Astrid's turn, the poor four-legged beast gets clubbed with Ursula's greatsword and Yakama's longsword.

I cringe. That's not exactly how we handle things at the animal shelter. The critter is probably just frightened. "You should at least see if he knows how to sit before you pull out your sword," I tell Ursula. She does some pretty good damage.

Jak goes next. Armando's eyes get sparkly and he rubs his hands together. This is the moment he's been waiting for. The princess is in the tower, waving her white hanky at him. Unfortunately, Jak's attack roll is so low he doesn't even get to roll for damage. Jak basically covered his eyes with one hand and swung his dagger with another. We tell him it's okay, because it is and it would be bad etiquette not to.

It appears we're doing nothing more than angering the beast—another animal shelter no-no. Teddy tells us the four-legged fiend is escaping over the railing. What do we do?

"Follow him!" Ursula shouts. "Everyone over the railing."

Everyone but Astrid, who is still on the piazza, shaking in her Jimmy Choos. "Can someone help me over the railing," I ask. "I'm wearing heels."

Helena, whose character probably did a triple somersault-back hand-spring off the railing, makes another face. She rolls her eyes more than her dice. "Just leave her up there," she says. "It's probably safer."

There has to be some rule in the etiquette handbook saying the use of reverse psychology on another player is really lame. It's the same crap my

Bad doggie!

trainer pulls when I tell him I'd rather have my intestines hand-fed to rats than do another set of bicep curls. That whole "we thought we raised you better than this" manipulation my parents pulled when they caught me swiping a can of cream ale before the eighth-grade dance. My dad later told me he was disappointed I didn't go for the good stuff. Hopefully Astrid hasn't learned by example, or she'll be spending this whole game hidden in the self-help section of Barnes and Noble.

Before I can prove Helena wrong, the hell hound gets a turn and exhales its fiery breath in Jak's direction. Our little rogue goes up in flames.

Jak screams. "Ahhhh! Please help me!"

"Stop, drop, and roll," Lucy tells him, and then corrects herself. "I mean, arrrgggg!" Ursula says instead.

"It's your turn, Astrid," Teddy says. He sounds regretful, like he's saying, "We don't have those in your size."

I quickly look over my weapons, trying to determine what will hurt the puppy least.

Amok grabs my character sheet. "Hit him with a *magic missile*," he says, making me wish I knew how to cast *mind your own freakin' business.*

"It's a dog!" I say. "I can't hurt an animal."

"It's a demon from another plane," Yakama volunteers. "Not a golden retriever."

"I'm on fire!" Jak screams. "Remember me?" Armando slaps his palms on the table for emphasis. Ironically the motion knocks mini-Astrid over.

"Can't walk in heels?" Tenoctris asks. She's smug for a woman whose own heels have never been more than six centimeters off the ground.

"Oh wow," I say. "Did someone cast sense of humor on her?"

"Fire!" Jak reminds us. "It's getting hot in here."

"Can I use my crossbow?" I ask Teddy. I think I might be metagaming but because I'm having a moral crisis and Jak is turning into a kabob, everyone lets it slide.

"You're out of range," Teddy explains. "You won't make it."

"Well, am I more than thirty feet from a Starbucks? Maybe I'll get a Frappuccino and wait for you guys."

Teddy calmly explains that I can either jump and get into the game or hold my action, meaning pass and hope man's best fiend takes off on its own accord. The eyes of my teammates are watching me. Helena's are seconds from rolling into her skull again. This isn't me, I remind myself. This is fantasy me. Astrid can do anything. She takes her shoes off and jumps into range and blasts the beast with a *magic missile*. I roll the appropriate die and Teddy tells me I did some real damage. I think I might cry. Hitting the pooch with a missile is almost as hard as bathing suit shopping in January.

"Good job, Astrid," Amok says, and he sounds sincere.

"He was going to kill us," Lucy says. "You did the right thing."

I'm not swayed until Hank says, "Pretend he ate your shoes."

The little furball turning my Jimmy Choos into Jimmy Chews? I don't think so!

With the help of Ursula's sword, Amok's spiritual weapon, Tenoctris's mad crazy fists, Yakama's mighty longsword, and even Jak's dagger, we take the hell hound down and snuff out the flames engulfing our friend. A cheer erupts in the room. Fists bang on the table. Teddy doles out experience points, not enough to get to the next level but I'm feeling very accomplished anyway.

Magic Missile

WORDS FOR WENCHES

You don't need to be a party-girl socialite to coin a new phrase. Just play a few rounds of D&D and you'll be spouting off in a new lingo in no time. In addition to "Dexterity" and "Initiative" and "melee touch attack" becoming part of your everyday vernacular, you may find yourself saying things in public only your gaming friends would understand.

✱ Teddy won't imitate a monstrous spider gasping its final breath, so it's all about word choice and inflection with him. If we do a little bit of damage he says, "You do damage." But if we really hit the sweet spot, he says, "You do *real* damage."

✱ When rolling to hit, we all know the higher the number, the better chance for success, right? So when a player in my group rolls anything over a seventeen we get all cocky and say, *"You totally hit."* Realizing we were on to something here, we decided to take "you totally hit" out of the dungeon conference room and into the conference room–conference room. When Armando was presenting the following year's media plans to the brand teams, Lucy told him he totally hit. When an editor came up with a new concept for a young adult book series, I told her that she totally hit. When Hank posted an email to the whole company thanking the executive team for hosting the company picnic, he said, "the bounce house totally hit" with his three year-old. Immediately he was called into Human Resources. Who hit his child? Was he hurt? Did he need legal council? Okay, maybe "you totally hit" is going to take a little longer to catch on than we thought. Or maybe one of us needs to host the Teen Choice Awards to make totally hit totally stick.

✱ *Buffing* or *buff* is another phrase with cross-universe appeal. To buff in D&D means something very similar in real life: Simply, casting spells to make yourself (or another character) stronger in skills or stats. To *buff* in the real world might mean getting a pedicure and having your eyebrows waxed and your roots dyed on a Friday afternoon to prepare you for the weekend. While *buff* is a verb in D&D, it's an adjective in the real world, and unfortunately there is no spell to achieve the desired affect of looking buff. How sad.

* A co-worker and fellow female roleplayer has been playing D&D for twenty years. She even met her husband through playing (more on that later). D&D vocabulary has infiltrated their everyday life in more ways than one. For instance, if Kim avoided tumbling off an uneven curb or getting pelted by pigeon poo, her husband would say "Looks like you made your saving throw." He might sneak up on her because he cast *"cat's grace"* (a buffing spell, by the way). And Kim's favorite fancy Pampered Chef baker is commonly referred to in their household as a *"+5 dish of baking."*

* *Rolling up a character* refers to the process of creating your character. You might say, "It took me four and a half months to roll up my character who ended up dying on our first adventure." I hope you don't end up saying that. Four months is a little extreme. I mean, how busy are you?

* *Tanking* or *to tank* is a common D&D phrase, meaning your most powerful character goes up front or in first. Like a tank. Get it? In the case of our game, Ursula acts as the tank. In context it might sound something like "You tank, Ursula, and we'll stay back here." In the real world tanking might mean sending one friend into a new club first to survey the scene before you all blow twenty bucks on a cover charge.

* By far the most disturbing D&D phrase I've heard is *TPK*, which stands for "total party kill." We're not talking "party kill" like the cops came and busted your kegger. We're talking about an encounter that leaves you and your entire party six feet under. According to Teddy, a DM doesn't strive to destroy his PCs, but almost any DM can recount on occasion where he or she scored a TPK. Is anyone else bothered by the use of the word *scored* as I am?

Somewhere in time before you or I had ever associated a dungeon with a dragon, someone was busy coining phrases that have now become the D&D lingua franca. Catch phrase or not, D&D is your world. You decide what totally hits.

Dungeon Decorum

You know the rules. Never wear white while adventuring after Labor Day. Don't cast spells with your mouth full. Keep your elbows off the play mat. You won't exactly lose hit points for doing any of these things, but you might lose favor with your group. It's all about manners, as that cardigan-wearing super-neighbor taught us.

In addition to your role in the party, you will likely have one of two roles *at* the party—host or guest. If you're a guest, exercise some common courtesy and follow these commandments of gaming.

Thou Shall Be on Time. It's not cool to leave your friends hanging, whether it's outside the multiplex or inside a dungeon fortress.

Thou Shall Not Bring Electronics to the Table. No cell phones, iPods, Blackberries, or Palm Pilots. Just turn the darn things off for a couple hours or if you must, keep them on vibrate. Nothing ruins the mood of a dungeon delve quicker than a muffled Justin Timberlake song coming from your pocket.

Thou Shall Not Litter. Don't leave your candy wrappers on the table, never use the upholstery to wipe the chocolate off your fingers, and please, people, never feed the family dog a piece of your Nestle Crunch. Do you have any idea how challenging it is to get a fourteen-year-old arthritic dog with digestive issues out of a third-story apartment? Even a 10th-level ranger would have trouble with that one.

Thou Shall Not Be Greedy. If you're a guest, offer to pitch in for delivery or bring enough snacks to share. Not everyone likes high-fiber cereal, but they love the chance to refuse it.

Thou Shall Be Courteous. Dungeon Mastering is a little bit like running a daycare. You have to keep everyone focused, happy, and entertained. You think they pull these adventures out of their hats? Maybe a little, but more than likely they spent a considerable amount of time preparing for your fun. The least you can do is say thank you.

Thou Shall Not Lose Focus. Keep your eye on the prize. Face to face with a carcass crab is probably not the best time to tell your friends about your date with the dentist you met at the grocery store.

Thou Shall Pay Attention. What? Sorry. I was text messaging the dentist.

Thou Shall Plan Ahead. No, not your next weekend retreat to the Oregon coast. Remember; eye on the prize! Always assume the beast will not be defeated by the time your turn rolls around again, so you should have your plan of attack ready and waiting.

Thou Shall Come Prepared. You wouldn't share your friend's deodorant or mascara, right? Well, if you do, you should stop. It's gross and unsanitary. Germs aside, you should also lay off your pal's D&D paraphernalia. When has a woman ever shunned an occasion to buy some new accessories? Exactly. So buck up and get your own pencils, set of dice, and *Player's Handbook*. And pick up some mascara, would you?

Thou Shall Not Flirt. Amok's flirting with Astrid is harmless, unless you count the bruises on his bicep from where she smacked him with her staff. But flirting at the table is disrespectful to your fellow gamers, not to mention awkward in a catching-your-parents-making-out sort of way. Excuse me while I go puke now.

Thou Shall Not Engage in Unnecessary Table Talk. Not only is table talk annoying to your fellow adventurers, it can be downright dangerous. Teddy tells a story about a group he DMs for that almost bit the dust because they were too busy chattering about last night's episode of *Lost* to check for traps. Guess what? The room they were entered was littered with *fireball* traps that dropped

Doting in the Dungeon

several PCs to 0 hit points instantly. You'd think once burned, twice shy, right? Nope. Still engrossed in tube time recaps, they missed all the hints Teddy was dropping about the trap recharging and managed to step into it yet again.

Thou Shall be a Good Host. If you're hosting, have some snacks and beverages on hand. Sure, your guests will probably bring something, but it always makes gamers feel at home when they're sitting next to a bowl of chips and salsa.

The Penguin Cometh

Ever get the feeling your friends are keeping something from you, and not in a surprise party sort of way? Astrid did something stupid after a particularly challenging encounter that resulted in Yakama, Jak, and Tenoctris being hypnotized into stabbing each other and speaking in incoherent babble (and yes, Tenoctris was much more social and enjoyable this way). Astrid was unscathed by the blowout, having cast most of her spells from a safe distance near the exit, but she was high on adrenaline. She used some spells she's never used before and quite frankly, we marveled at their competence. We were looking for a magical sword and we found it after defeating the dastardly beast who owned it. It was just lying on the ground (for good reason) and well, it was magical. Not all magic is good magic, as Astrid soon learned. She went right for the sword and hoisted it in the air.

The rest of the party became my own Greek chorus. "No! Drop it! Are you stupid?"

Naturally, I assumed they were talking to Jak. Clearly Astrid hadn't done anything wrong. It wasn't until Teddy called me out of the room that I realized Astrid might have made a very big mistake. Being asked to step outside with the Dungeon Master is much worse than being called out of homeroom to go see the principal. I realized this was why my mom doesn't like phone calls after 10:00 PM. I was sure I was about to hear some very bad news about my baby elf.

Astrid wasn't dead, but she had been possessed by the sword and the darn thing was using her to take it where it wanted to go. It was like an evil hitchhiker riding shotgun, pressing a loaded revolver into my ribcage. *Take me to Santa Fe! Stop at the next Jack in the Box!* I was out in the hall, arguing with the sword, a.k.a. Teddy, while it was telling me what to do. The sword promised a handsome reward.

"Do you want to be rich?"

"Yes."

"Then do as I tell you."

"Okay."

Leaving my group unattended had given them plenty of time to debate Astrid's fate. Reentering the room, I notice Astrid the mini at the far end of the play mat while her fellow adventurers huddle in the farthest corner.

"Is it a *penguin*?" Yakama asks.

"We shouldn't take our chances," Tenoctris says. "Penguins are dangerous."

"Now there are penguins in this game?" I ask. Come on! Even Astrid wouldn't run away from a little penguin. They can't even fly. I continue with my mission. "I think we should go to Karrnath to return the sword. We should help the sword reach its final destination and be handsomely rewarded for our efforts."

"It's a penguin," Amok says. "Definitely a penguin."

"Do it!" Tenoctris demands. "Get rid of the penguin!"

"What freakin' penguin?" I shout. And I thought I was the one possessed.

"*That* penguin!" Yakama shouts.

With that the rest of the group ducks while Yakama casts *entangle*, a 1st-level spell that causes creatures, or in this case yours truly, to be entwined in weeds, bushes, trees, you name it. If it grows outside and could potentially house a tick or a red robin, it's on, around, and squeezing the evil demons out of Astrid like an environmentally friendly exorcism. This is why I don't camp, hike, or even park my car in the shade. Nature is evil! It's Jack and Beanstalk gone wild.

Turns out that for my group, *penguin* is a code word for a friend who is potentially dangerous and must be stopped.

"We can't trust you if you're hypnotized by the sword. What if you turn on us?" To her credit, Ursula sounds genuinely sad.

"Hypnosis isn't all bad. What if I were trying to quit smoking or curb my sweet tooth?" I counter. But it's no use. They keep me wrapped up in vines until the spell I'm under wears off twenty-four D&D hours later (about a game and a half for us). At least I don't have to worry about going first in combat.

Dear Diary,

Why can't I ever have a nice, relaxing day? My feet are killing me, I've got calluses the size of silver pieces, and I'm more tired than a horde of zombies. All I want is a hot bath and a pedicure. Okay, and maybe a massage. Instead, I got embroiled in a beat down with a cloaker. Talk about being at the wrong place at the wrong time. Now I see why my mom said Ursula was a bad influence.

Anyway, it happened like this. We met up with the guys because Jak scored invitations to this hot new club called Temple. Clubs aren't really my scene. In fact, I can't really picture any of us as the clubbing types except maybe Amok, since no matter what he says it always sounds like he's saying it from a barstool with an apple martini in his hand. But I had a few hours to kill before my kickboxing class, so what the heck? At the very least it would be fun to watch Tenoctris be denied entry because she looks like she's dressed in the MC Hammer yoga collection. She's so last season. Oh yeah, she was there too. She follows Yakama around like a bad reputation.

Jak insisted he knew where we were going, but close to three miles later we began to doubt him. That's when Tenoctris took over the lead, believing she knew right where to go. She did too, if we wanted to go to a real temple as opposed to a club called Temple.

Talk about literal. I wonder where she thinks the Stork Club is. No time to argue because wouldn't you know it? The sky opened up and we were suddenly getting pummeled with rain and hail.

"Everyone inside!" Yakama ordered, which was simply brilliant. I mean, I'd probably still be standing there with my stilettos mired in mud if he hadn't suggested we take cover. Sorry—I'm just bitter because I missed kickboxing and the first twenty minutes of Project Runway.

The temple appeared deserted and creepy. It felt like we weren't alone and a shiver ran down my spine.

"Do you hear that?" Jak asked, and I could only assume he was referring to the distinct low, mournful wail. Everyone was visibly shaken. Rain be damned, I thought. I'll sacrifice my shoes and three more pairs rather than have to face what we knew was lurking behind the shadows! But it was too late. From behind one of the columns, a cloaker appeared. A cloaker is a clever mantalike beast that gets its name from its black wings that resemble a cloak when resting. It wasted no time swooping down and engulfing Tenoctris in those very mighty black wings.

"Holy hell hounds!" Jak yelled. "It's got Tenoctris!" Hey, thanks for the play-by-play.

Yakama pulled out his longsword. Ursula already had her greatsword in hand.

"Stab it!" Amok yelled, ready to back them up with his heavy mace.

Ursula sent a mighty thrust through one scaly black wing.

"Owwwwww!" we heard from within.

Jak went next. He shot. He scored!

"Wahhhhhhhh!" It's true cloakers emit creepy, mournful howls that are enough to knock even the strongest warrior off kilter, but this was something new all together. These sounds were almost . . . human?

Yakama stabbed the beast one more time and this time we heard, "Help me!" I didn't think cloakers could speak.

They can't! That was Tenoctris in there calling for help. But come on! What did she think we were doing? We were stabbing as fast as possible.

Just as Ursula was about to go back for seconds, Amok told everyone to hold up. "We're stabbing Tenoctris!"

The cloaker had Tenoctris in such a tight grip that she couldn't manage to shape-shift. She was stuck inside, suffering numerous bites and stabs and losing strength by the millisecond. Yikes. Normally I'd pay money to see something like this happen to someone like her, but even I felt bad. We'd practically turned the girl into a

Jackson Pollack painting. I made up for my
ill wishes by nailing the beast with a couple
of magic missiles.

Amok attempted to club the beast over
its head, doing a small amount of damage
but still, the death grip remained. Yakama
shot his longbow and got the cloaker square
in the forehead. I cast ray of exhaustion.
I'm new at this one, having only practiced
a few times, but I must be a natural. The
beast was immediately exhausted, giving
Ursula a clear shot with her greatsword. It
loosened its grip enough for Tenoctris to
slip out from underneath. She was pretty
beaten up but we didn't have much time to
heal her before the spell ended. Yakama and
Jak finished the cloaker off, stabbing it
several times in the head while the rest of
us rushed outside. Who knows if there might
have been more cloakers inside? Amok cast
cure moderate wounds and Tenoctris regained
her strength. We decided we'd had enough
excitement for one night and headed home.
That was probably a better workout than
my kickboxing class.

It's weird. If I weren't with my friends, I
never would have gotten into that mess. But
if I weren't with them, I never would have
gotten out of it. I guess it's a fair trade.

Tomorrow I'm definitely getting a massage.
Love, Astrid

FOOD FOR THOUGHT

Impress your friends and get everyone in the mood for some good old-fashioned monster hunting. Below is a sample menu when hosting your first D&D surprise party. Word to the wise: Try not to serve messy finger foods that could drip onto the play mat and get your dice all sticky. Sloppy dice, drink twice. Oh wait—that's a different game.

Cocktails: Awaken the dead with any of the following concoctions:

✳ *Bloody Mary*
✳ *Black Martini*
✳ *Vampire Kiss*

Starters: Kick that metabolism into high gear and get ready for adventure with these fine palate teasers:

✳ *Seven Player Dip*
✳ *Magic Mushroom Pizzettes*
✳ *Dragon Fire Salsa*
✳ *Hellish Hummus with Pita Chips*
✳ *Dungeon Delving Dill Dip*
✳ *Holy Guacamole with Garlic Tortilla Spikes*
✳ *Glitterdust Ball o' Cheese*
✳ *Zombified Zucchini Bites*
✳ *Deviled Egg Spread on Herbed Crostinis*
✳ *Halflings in a Blanket*

Entrees: All that dodging and ducking calls for some serious carbs and protein. Boost your strength the natural way with these hearty treats:

✳ *Man-It-Got-Me Manicotti!*
✳ *Magic Missile Meatballs (see p. 130)*
✳ *Tandoori Chicken (or is it?) Spears*
✳ *Steamed Artichoke the Monster with Garlic Butter Dip*
✳ *Initiative Rolls with Herbed Olive Oil (see p. 134)*

Desserts: Success may smell sweet, but these treats are sweeter. Celebrate victory or treat defeat with these delicious confections:

✳ *Red Devil's Food Cupcakes*
✳ *Angel Food Cake with Midnight Berries and Wine*

Hold person: Keep Mr. Grubby from becoming Mr. Grabby

Chapter Five

WHERE'S THE PARTY?

Think geeking out with the girls on a Friday night sounds like an activity you might enjoy? Great. Now what? If you don't have a game and an experienced DM literally at your fingertips, fear not. There's probably a game being played near you right now.

Joining a D&D group is similar to joining a poker game or a writer's group or a knitting circle. Actually, I have no idea if it's similar to a knitting circle, but I like the visual comparison of the two in my head. ("I'd like to cast-on for one-by-one ribbing, please.") The point is, these groups already exist, so all you need to start rolling is to pull up a chair.

But how do you find these elusive groups, you ask? It's not like D&D is played on Astroturf in broad daylight. Here are some tips:

Boys First. Chances are at least one guy you know played D&D when he was a kid. Know that friend who has superhero action figures on his bookshelves and high-concept art made out of Legos? Yeah. Start with him. No doubt he has some slain skeletons crammed in his closet next to the *Star Wars* t-shirts and comic book lending library. He'll probably regale you with tales of his D&D adventures. How he and his two best friends used to spend entire summers camped out in their basement crafting their own adventures. Most likely he'll be tickled with the thought that you'd like to slay a few dragons by his side. Readers beware: If he doesn't already have a crush on you, this will most likely seal the deal. Be a warforging vixen on the play mat but be gentle off. Rejection stings no matter how many hit points you have.

If you don't have any friends who will cop to being D&D players in their youth, they're probably lying, and you wouldn't want to adventure with someone you can't trust, right?

Join the Club. Ah, the life of the matriculated. Discounts on youth hostels and the lack of common sense not to stay at one. Those were the days. Actually no, they weren't. Someone stole my Walkman from a hostel in Belgium and my friend got ringworm from the sheets. Thus my love affair with four-star hotels began. Excuse the tangent. We were talking about students for a reason. They often belong to clubs and college campuses usually have gaming clubs. If you are a student, you might try joining or starting a D&D club. It's cool! It's vintage! If you're not a student, please don't try this on a college campus. People will start rumors. In fact, I will start rumors.

What's in Store? Sorry, Nordstrom isn't likely to hold gaming groups anytime soon. Too bad, because I could roleplay a socialite spendthrift pretty much everyday. But there are some better retail options if you're looking for an existing group or the means to start your own. Behold: the gaming shop. Chock full of trading cards, action figures, comic books, oh my! Maybe you've walked past it quickly on your way to get your nails done. Or maybe you've dropped your little brother off there while you were getting your nails done. Regardless, it's a great place to meet other gamers. Walking in there is also a great self-esteem boost. You'll feel like the homecoming queen in the middle of an A/V club meeting.

Log On. Mom's been telling you for years that meeting people online is the wave of the future. She even gave you a three-month subscription to one of the Internet's most popular sites. Or maybe that's just my mom. Kudos to her for thinking it would only take three months to find the love of my life, but to be honest, I really would have liked a Kitchen Aid mixer or a spa gift certificate instead.

If lovebirds can find their one true mate online by simply typing in their zip codes, you can find a group of adventurers willing to storm the castle with you simply by doing a search online. You'll find about a zillion resources by doing a search, but a good place to start is **www.wizards.com/community**. You'll find plenty of D&D players looking for new players to join an existing group or someone eager to start a new group.

Another great resource is the Roleplaying Gamers Association (or RPGA). Yep, you guessed it, the RPGA is an organization for roleplaying gamers, offering fans a chance to hook up with other gamers and get playing tips, free adventures, and rewards for playing. It's your favorite grocery store's membership club on steroids.

When carousing around online, don't forget—these are strangers and you're a nice girl. Please use caution when meeting people online. If someone tells you he's relaxing in his tower wearing nothing but stilettos and a barbed wire teddy, he probably is. And never, ever do an online search for "dungeons." Especially at work. Just trust me, okay?

Members Only

A *DUNGEONS & DRAGONS* game group is only as good as its members and its members are best in small numbers. If you are denied entry into a local D&D game, don't take it personally. It's kind of like that annoying rule at beer gardens and popular clubs: No one can enter until someone else leaves. Too may gamers around the table can spoil the fun. Just think, if there are fifteen people playing, the beast could be slain before you even get a turn. All that prepping of spells and loading of crossbows for nothing! It's best to keep it intimate with six, maybe seven players maximum.

SOCIAL STUDIES

You've heard the expression "show, don't tell," right? I thought I'd heed that advice when it comes to pledging my allegiance to *DUNGEONS & DRAGONS*.

The Mission: Sport a nifty *DUNGEONS & DRAGONS* t-shirt while hanging out in a beer garden at a busy outdoor festival.

Observations: Definitely noticed some double takes and furrowed eyebrows. Even got one guy nudging his friend and pointing.

Result: Inconclusive. After forty-five minutes of people staring at my chest and pointing, insecurity got the best of me and I gave my friend twenty bucks to borrow her sweatshirt. Perhaps I'll stick to "telling."

And intimate it is. Membership in a D&D group is more privileged than Donald Trump's offspring. *DUNGEONS & DRAGONS* games tend to be weekly, and the members are dedicated. It sucks to go out into the big bad wild without your cleric, and playing the absentee guy's character plus your own is just too much responsibility for some. Again, don't take it personally if your application is turned down. Nothing against your juju, it could just be that the group's existing vibe may be too good to mess with.

If you're the kind of person who doesn't like to be told no, perhaps it's best you start your own game. You can search for a Dungeon Master the same as you would players or a group looking for new members. Start with your friends, and if no one is willing to cop to any priors DM-ing, move on. Fill your group with friends, or anyone whose life you wouldn't mind saving. If you have an experienced DM, you can all be new to DUNGEONS & DRAGONS. It's almost more fun to start out that way.

Mastering Your Domain

Ever been called a control freak? Ever been called a control freak and didn't see it as a negative? Do you like telling people what to do? Do you make the dinner reservations and seek out the best beach house rentals? Do most of your sentences start off with "you should"? Do you know the singular best way to make a pomegranate martini? Does it piss you off when friends don't heed your fashion advice? Do you sometimes wish you could send your pals into a dark, dank dungeon with only a handful of tindertwigs and a miner's pick and drop a platoon of dire rats in their path? Then you, my scheming and somewhat scary sister, have all the makings of a wonderful Dungeon Master.

Some might argue that the Dungeon Master is the most important element of a D&D game. Without a DM, there'd be a handful of players sitting around a table doing a whole lot of nothing. Yeah, I guess it's important. The Dungeon Master is equivalent to the soap opera writer. If he or she is good at the job—telling stories, creating villains, turning every day player characters into heroes, building a descriptive world, and filling it with rich, engaging supportive characters—everyone has a jolly old time and your character looks good. It can be a thankless job, or at least one that remains shadowed by the egomaniac, pumped up, supercharged PCs who get to reap the rewards of the DM's hard work. But if you're a good Dungeon Master, that's okay. When I asked Teddy why he enjoyed being a Dungeon Master, he said that he loves telling stories and introducing people to the world of DUNGEONS & DRAGONS. I said that might be true of other groups, but does he really like DM-ing our unruly group? He said, "especially" our group. Why? Because for the most part, we're all new and we ask a lot of questions. Our characters are fresh-faced and just coming into their personalities like babies who discover the softness of chenille and musical choo choo trains for the first time. Sometimes we take stupid risks, sometimes someone finds a new way to get out of a ziggurat, and we always feel very accomplished when we successfully complete an adventure. He didn't mention my spells' sound effects as a reason, but I'm pretty sure that goes without saying.

After a particularly exciting adventure, my game group disbands with all the giddy, red-faced joy of kids coming off of a loop-de-loop roller coaster. I dare say some of us have popped a blood vessel or two and broken out into a cold sweat toward the end of a session. We thank Teddy, tell him he did a great job, and can't wait for next week. As he packs up his cardboard screen and dumps filtered water from his name brand plastic bottle onto the play mat and wipes off the remains of that day's adventure, I see him smile. Mission accomplished. He led his players on a fun-filled, victorious escapade. And on Wednesday when we're still talking about it, or plotting how we'll escape the train loaded with vampire foes next time, Teddy sits facing his computer screen, diligent and straight backed, not giving away that he's listening until we see his shoulders quiver and head drop. He's laughing at us, metagaming all over the company—in conference rooms, kitchens, the company gym. "I should have used my sword." "We looted three bottles of cure light wounds potions." "I could have used mage hand to dump holy water on his crotch." The game's been over for days, but still we can't stop talking about it.

A Dungeon Master "runs" a DUNGEONS & DRAGONS game. It's like running a movie theater or running the entire country. He or she is in charge. Sounds enticing, sure. What would you do if you ran the world? Free health care? Give M&Ms their own level on the food pyramid? Dungeon Mastering is no small feat. There's a lot of work that goes into it. It's like cramming for the SATs every single week. You'll need to decide what obstacles your PCs will face and how they can overcome those challenges. What danger awaits them as they embark on their path? What will the reward be? You can make up your own story entirely, or feel free to run a pre-made adventure that you can pick up at your local hobby store or download online.

You also need to decide what kind of Dungeon Master you want to be. This is important because you'll get a reputation quicker than my friend Jackie in sixth grade after she made out with seven boys, including the DJ, at the Thanksgiving dance. We know who those guys were giving thanks to the next night at dinner.

Remember in college when you were deciding what classes to take and you asked around about what the teachers were like? Never mind what the class was actually about. Do the teachers tolerate lateness? How are they as lecturers? Will you get extra credit if you wash her car or pick up his dry cleaning? People will talk about your Dungeon Mastering skills and compare you to others. When Teddy told us he'd be gone for nearly a month on vacation, my group decided to look for "guest Dungeon Masters" each week. Finding subs wasn't difficult. I can't shake a staff without hitting several willing and qualified candidates. Choosing one wasn't so easy. I heard about Dungeon Masters who were "mean," "hard," "too serious," "boring," and "notorious for knocking off at least one character a game." Um, no. Maybe we'd just wait for Teddy to get back.

Master Class

So what makes a good Dungeon Master? The obvious answers would be a love of the game, knowledge of the rules, and the ability to spin a good tale. A good DM also possesses the following skills.

Play to the Players. Get to know your players and prep the adventure based on that knowledge. If you're DM'ing for a group of animal rights activists and you know even knocking off a swarm of beetles will be painful for them, maybe it's better to bring them face to face with vampires and skeletons.

Help History Repeat Itself. If your players have thoroughly filled out their character sheets and written novellas worth of backstories, utilize their history to add depth to your adventures.

Don't Antagonize. A good Dungeon Master realizes that storytelling is a solo job, but building the story you tell is a group effort. Involve your players in the process. And if the players take the story in a different direction than you imagined, it's okay to gently steer them back in the "right" direction. Remember, you can "force" a character, but you can't force a player.

Be Honest. If you want to run an urban adventure that takes place in a city where magic is frowned upon and drunken brawling is prohibited, make sure your spell-tossing, aggressive types know this in advance. Anything the characters would know, it's a good idea to share with the players.

Storming Your Castle

Want to treat your girlfriends to an evening of *Dungeons & Dragons*? Great idea! But having gone there myself, allow me to impart some advice on how to do it up nice.

First rule: Make it a surprise. People are much more inclined to participate in something they normally wouldn't want to if they have no idea they're going to do it. After high school and a particularly traumatizing gym class, I promised my athletically challenged self I'd never hold a baseball bat again unless it was for self defense. Several years later I found myself swinging the old white ash stick at friend's four-year-old's birthday party, banging the snot out of a paper maché SpongeBob. Hey, there were Butterfingers inside, and if I left it up to little Tyler, he'd be able to drive to the store and buy me a bag before he busted that thing open. The point is, much to my surprise, when the bat actually makes contact with something, it can be kind of fun.

It was important to me to test out my theory: Can a woman outside the typical gamer profile learn to enjoy a game like *Dungeons & Dragons*? I went right to the source, asking a nongamer girlfriend if she wanted to come over next Friday for some dinner and a game of *Dungeons & Dragons*. Her response? Nothing. Crickets. Just a look muddled somewhere between astounded and repulsed.

"What's your problem?" I asked. "Hasn't anyone ever asked you to dinner?" Her look sharpened, which made me think perhaps no one has.

Finally she responded, "Did you just ask me to play *Dungeons & Dragons*?"

"No," I said, trying to salvage our friendship. I had no idea she was so fragile. "I said, 'Do you want to come over for dinner and drink *tons of gin on my wagon?*'" Wow, I was really stretching but she bought it.

"I hate gin," she said. "But the wagon sounds cool."

This brings us to our second rule of thumb: Be selective with your invite list. Not everyone is open to the wide world of dungeon diving. Stereotypes are alive and well, especially to women whose geeky brothers played D&D or who didn't know anyone who played but used it as an insult for boys they disliked. *"Why don't you go back to your basement and play* Dungeons & Dragons?*"* is right up there with *"You're so hideous your parents should have named you Fugly."*

Think about your friends as your fellow adventurers. How important it is to have a well-rounded group. You can't all be afraid of heights or inept with weapons. Someone needs to be able to kick the dung out of a pack of bugbears without dissolving into a fit of righteousness.

Remember those women from my informal focus group? The ones gracious enough to share their impressions of *DUNGEONS & DRAGONS*? I decided they were primed and ready to take a stab at stabbing the dragon themselves. Plus, I wanted to try my hand at Dungeon Mastering and figured it was best to practice with a bunch of newbies who had no idea their characters aren't supposed to bite it and reincarnate after every round.

Neglecting to share my true intentions for the evening, I invited them over for an evening of dinner and drinks, which essentially is D&D. That brings us to our third rule for throwing a D&D party: Lie. Or rather, leave out some of the details. Sure, you'll provide food and libations. Maybe even have a few more games on tap for the evening—poker, Scrabble, good old-fashioned Truth or Dare and Would You Rather. *Would you rather date a guy who wore Kiss cologne or played* Dungeons & Dragons?

Every good hostess worth her matching salt and pepper shakers knows what you serve is just as important as who you're serving it to. The fourth rule for a successful D&D party? Menu planning. No, you don't need to match the perfect wine with every course or even serve courses, but the wine will definitely help. I decided to theme my gathering "Minis and Martinis," which only made my friends angry because they thought I was downsizing their drinks. It really helps your D&D party if your friends are a bunch of lushes.

Speaking of lushy friends, before the evening rolled around I asked them if they thought they would ever play DUNGEONS & DRAGONS.

Subject A: From what I know—no. The main reason is that I think you have to have D&D friends, and I don't. It also seems too complicated, like when someone tries to teach you a card game and there are so many rules that before you have your first round dealt, you have already had three beers.

Subject B: If I had a group of D&D virgins, I might try it.

Subject C: Probably not. It seems too complicated and I'm too old to learn something with so many rules.

Subject D: Only if there were a cash prize involved.

Subject E: Good question, I don't know . . . I've never considered myself a "role play" type of gal. Maybe if I knew more about the game and less hearsay, I would give it a shot, but I refuse to become one of those basement gamer geeks!

Can't say their answers were too surprising. Again, they'd all come to the same conclusion that D&D is "hard" and you need to have a basement and a secret handshake to learn it. I have none of those things, but I do have high hopes that I'll be blowing all of their stereotypes out of the water.

Drunkards and Dragons

To get everyone in the mood for what they didn't know they were in for, I tailored my menu to suit my cause. Mini pizzas, mini quiches, mini cupcakes dotted with mini chocolate chips. And those were just the appetizers. Contrary to my friends' misconceptions, the martinis were not mini. *That* was essential. For more menu suggestions, see the sidebar on page 116.

The martinis were flowing, the appetizers were gone, the mini cupcakes had left mini chocolate mustaches over our top lips. No one cared. We were having a wonderful time. There is something to be said for having an authentic "girl's night in." No topic is off limits and no one will judge you if you confess to reading your boyfriend's email when he's in the shower.

"He left it open!"

"He must have wanted you to read it!"

"You'd have to read it to determine its importance before you closed it."

"Wouldn't want to lose any half-written emails."

That's teamwork!

And the dating stories from the front lines—the beasts women encounter every day. The cling-on, the juggler, the bad manners guy. Prospective suitors have kids, limited vocabularies, ex-girlfriends in the not so distant past. We weed our way through first dates like a tourist through the African bush. All this just to get to the hacking-into-email account phase? *That's* combat!

Maybe it was the martinis clouding my judgment, but I started to feel confident the girls weren't going to mind the ambush attack and would enjoy playing D&D. A few of them do play games—Uno, Cranium, Poker. They bet in *Survivor* pools. One even auditioned to be on *Survivor*. There's no way they can't love this game! Still, as the witching hour approaches, I get a little nervous. What if they hate it? What if they hate me for making them play? What if they wait for me in the parking lot tomorrow morning and kick my ass on my way to my car? Okay, it's definitely the martinis talking. We're all grown women in our twenties and thirties. I'm asking them to play a game, not donate a kidney.

Just in case, I get up and lock the door. Then I move a chair in front of it. Casually I shove my desk in front of the chair.

"What are you doing?" Subject A asks. "Is someone out there? Is someone after us?" She's getting visibly panicked and I feel bad. I forgot vodka makes her paranoid. At least in perspective, asking her to don the robes of a rogue won't seem so horrible.

Subject D is much more relaxed. "Suddenly we're in a *Lifetime* TV movie. Who's out there? Meredith Baxter Birney? Valerie Bertinelli?"

"Ooh. She wants revenge! " Subject B is giddy. I had no idea she even knew what *Lifetime* television was. "What have you done? Stolen her husband?"

"No, her teenage daughter," Subject C offers.

Subject E is about three seconds shy of writing a screenplay. "No, her daughter's husband and the family farm. You met when you showed up from the city bank to foreclose on the property. Now they have nothing! You're a farm-wrecker."

Whether it's the thought of me living it up on a stolen farm, me actually being able to steal someone's husband, or Mrs. Keaton outside my barricaded door demanding retribution, my friends are in stitches. Perhaps now is a good time to pull out the Basic Game. They very clearly have no trouble delving into fantasyland.

"Okay," I say, moving to a position of authority at the head of the table. I'm feeling very much like my elementary school librarian, who unsuccessfully tried to get our attention by clapping her hands three times. Didn't work for her and it wasn't going to work for me. "I have to confess. I had an ulterior motive for inviting you all here." "Ulterior motive" gets the *Lifetime* television-addicted crowd's attention.

Unwilling to wait for an explanation, they come up with their own. Of course.

"You're moving."

"You're getting married."

"You're getting married to Valerie Bertinelli's daughter's husband and moving to a farm?"

Cue exploding laughter.

Curses! The stupid farm set them off again. All right, I'm not the most outdoors-y person—I think we covered that—but I do love animals. Why is it so hard to see me on a farm?

"None of the above," I say. I'm back in control. They're feeling playful, more than half drunk, and I haven't given them dessert yet. They're putty in my hands. "I invited you here to play a little game."

Silence.

"Didn't you hear me?" I ask. "We're playing a game. Games are fun. You like games, right?"

Mama Makes a Mean Magic Missile Meatball. And now you can too. Just like magic missiles, these little orbs of delight can't miss.

Here's how to make your own batch.

Toss the following into a crockpot:
1 bag of frozen meatballs (veggie meatballs work well too)
1 jar of chili sauce
1 jar of grape jelly

Crock away for four hours and viola! You're the new Betty Crocker.

Subject D speaks first. "What kind of game?"

"You're going to kill us, aren't you?" Subject A asks, backing her chair into the corner. She might as well hand me a baseball bat and duct tape her arms to her sides.

"No, of course not," I say, taking her martini away.

"You want us to kill each other?" Subject B asks, much calmer than I'd expect someone who was asking that question to be.

"That really was a movie," Subject E adds. "I always said she watched too much TV."

Me? I think. I'm not the one sitting here storyboarding television's next movie of the week.

"You're being ridiculous," I say. "I don't want to kill you. I want to teach you how to play a game." I toss the Basic Game on the table and let the box do the talking for me.

My friends move in closer, curious, like they've just unearthed some secret treasure.

"*DUNGEONS & DRAGONS*?"

Realization sets in and they recoil back like the darn thing bared its teeth at them. The only sound I hear is that of Subject B trying to choke back sobs. It's like someone cast *repulsion* in here. Finally someone speaks.

"Ew!"

"What the. . . ."

"Are you in some kind of a cult?" Subject D asks. "Do you need to recruit five more people into your secret web of dragon slaying before you can win a toaster?"

"Oh no, you drank the Kool-Aid!" Subject E shouts. "I knew it was only a matter of time before the Wizards finally got to you."

Subject B is hesitant but sympathetic. "I thought my job was bad when they made us do karaoke at the Christmas party."

And here I was thinking the martinis were going to help. My friends are hostile, slurring, beer-muscling leaders. "No one is making me teach you. I do not win home appliances and I haven't drunk Kool-Aid in twenty-six years. I'm teaching you how to play *DUNGEONS & DRAGONS* because I honestly think you'll like it."

There is a pause where I think they finally get it. Maybe not looking forward to it, but resigned to it.

Subject A speaks first. "Is it really this hard to meet guys the normal way? What about Match.com? I'll buy your first month."

"Mom already did, and nope, not trying to meet guys. If you don't play with me right now you will forfeit your mini-molten chocolate lava cake with organic raspberries, homemade fudge sauce, and vanilla-tinged whipped cream. Your call."

Finally they've been beaten. I should feel bad using such an obvious tactic, but I don't. Chocolate is a more powerful weapon than a masterwork two-bladed sword.

"If we promise to play, can we have our dessert first?" Subject B asks.

"No."

"Can we have it *while* we play?" Subject C asks.

"No." I open the box and start handing out game pieces. Thank the D&D gods for the Basic Game, which comes equipped with everything new players need to start playing: minis, monsters, dice, pre-made character sheets, simple instructions, and a ready-made adventure yours truly will be leading her lemmings—I mean friends—on.

Basic Game characters are a well-rounded bunch. You've got your sorcerer, rogue, cleric, and fighter—all of different races. The obvious choice for Lidda the badass, browbeating halfling rogue would be Subject D, but that wouldn't involve uncharacteristic roleplaying for her, so I give the part to Subject E. Regdar the human fighter goes to Subject A. I don't want to stretch her imagination too far by making her play a dwarf or a gnome. Subject C gets to play Eberk, the dwarf cleric because she's the shortest of the bunch (I know, I know, typecasting but. . . .) and I let Subjects B and D tag-team the part of Aramil, the elf sorcerer. Subject B is too fragile to play her own character and Subject D could use some refining around the edges from the elven culture.

I give them a moment to read through their character sheets before realizing they have no idea what any of this means. Armor class? Hit points? Initiative? As foreign as *gradisco mangiare il* (which means *I like tacos* in Italian).

"Okay, ladies," I begin.

"We're not ladies," Subject B interjects. "At least I don't think we are. Are we?" She holds up Aramil's character sheet.

"No, you're a man. My bad. Okay, ladies and gentlemen—"

"Are you sure we're not a woman?" Subject D asks. "I mean, look at the hair. And the delicate facial figures."

Subject C looks over her shoulder. "You're a dude. Look at those biceps. And he's wearing cap sleeves. A woman would know capped sleeves and large upper arms is a big fashion faux pas. He's showing off."

"You're a guy," I say, pointing to the character description that blatantly says "he."

"Fine," Subject B says, looking dejected. "I thought this game was about fantasy and making up your own characters."

Subject E sighs, reminding us she's still here. "I guess our fate has been predetermined. Just like real life. It's so demoralizing."

I've always found her a bit lazy and lax when it comes to making decisions regarding her future. Now I know why. Maybe I shouldn't have let her take the role of the fighter.

I need to get this game going before my buzz wears off, so I concede that Aramil is a woman with large biceps and bad fashion sense.

I have them take out their minis and use the time while they're cooing over their "little, tiny people" to refill their drinks. I fill Subject A's glass with Bud Light.

"My guy looks so angry," Subject C comments, regarding Eberk. "Not very dwarf-like."

"How do you know what dwarves are like?" Subject D asks. I'm glad I'm not the only one she pesters.

"Everyone knows what dwarves are like," Subject C answers. "Have you never been to a mall at Christmas?"

"Those are elves," we all say. Calling out your friend's stupidity in unison—now that's teamwork! Subject D, of course, adds a *dumbass* in there.

"We've got the elf," Subject B says, holding up her character sheet. "But he's a far cry from Herbie the dentist from Rudolph."

Once I went to a Bon Jovi concert with binoculars that had only one lens. I think those glasses had better focus than this group. I'm getting a hangover waiting for them to concentrate, not to mention heading for a major sugar crash. Whose stupid rule was it not to have dessert until we finished?

I try to channel Teddy and realize he has the same problem keeping our group reigned in. Instead I try channeling the mistress of captive audiences—Oprah.

This is How We Roll

You can't go wrong with cooked dough and butter, but here's a foolproof way to make your guests believe your pretty little fingers are exhausted from kneading dough all day. (Or at least that you drove five miles out of your way to the really good bakery.)

Initiative Rolls

1 package (or more) of refrigerated dinner rolls
4–6 oz of Gorgonzola cheese
1/4 teaspoon of dried herbs such as rosemary or oregano
2–3 tablespoon of chopped walnuts

Bake rolls according to directions. Mix cheese, herbs, and nuts together. Let rolls cool 5 minutes before squishing cheese mixture into center of rolls. Bake for 2–4 more minutes or until cheese begins to melt.

Serve warm with a nice bottle of already-herbed olive oil, or be adventurous and add your own herbs to plain extra-virgin olive oil. Dunk away!

"All right, let's get this party started. You're on a quest to find hot molten lava cakes before the whipped cream is dried up."

It's working! Oprah is in the house! They stop chattering and comparing miniatures and talking about Aramil's widow's peak and Lidda's huge quads. They're actually looking right at me, waiting for something to happen.

Do something! Oprah commands. Your captive audience won't stay spellbound for long.

"Right. Put your minis on the play mat."

They do as told and all eyes return to me. In the Basic Game, there is no rolling for initiative. Initiative scores are predetermined. I ask each of them to check their character sheet to see who has the highest.

"Lidda has seventeen," Subject E says. She sounds like she's talking about her daughter who made the honor roll. "That's good, right?"

"That's great," I say, picturing my dumb but burly kid beating hers up on the playground. "So good that you get to go first."

"Nice job, Thunder Thighs," Subject D commends.

"Typical," Subject A says. "Leave it to the woman to take the initiative while the boys hang back and program their TiVos."

We set up the dungeon tiles (also part of the Basic Game) and I begin the adventure. "Lizard creatures called kobolds attacked the local baron while he was out hunting. He escaped, but the little bastards stole his ring."

Silence.

"I mean, his dessert. His entire molten chocolate lava cake factory."

"How do you steal an entire factory?"

At least they're paying attention. This is what I get for ad-libbing my first adventure. "They just took it over," I say, hoping they'll let it go.

"They're tiny lizard people," Subject E says. "You mean this big tough king couldn't handle a few lizards? Even I wouldn't be afraid of them."

"Oh, you would too," Subject B reminds her. "You practically peed your pants at the butterfly exhibit at the zoo."

"I didn't say they were small. And they're powerful. And there's lots of them." She doesn't seem convinced so I add the ever persuasive, "Just go with it!"

"I'd be afraid of lizard people," Subject B says, winking at me. "I had a next door neighbor growing up who looked like a lizard and I was terrified to even walk past her house."

I continue. "You've heard kobolds hang out near some old ruins that were once an alchemist's secret laboratory." I look up from the adventure and am nothing short of amazed. They're actually paying attention. They can't take their eyes off me. I'm mentally beer-muscling and feel confident enough to veer off my script yet again. "The alchemist has been M.I.A. for years, presumed dead by the evil beasts that inhabit the dungeon. DANGER IS ALL AROUND YOU! But you, my friends, you are strong and fearless adventurers and you're ready to kick some kobold butt."

Maybe the spirit of Oprah really is running through my veins because it's been four and a half minutes and my friends haven't launched into one tangent or told me how stupid I am for withholding their dessert until they play a stupid game with me. Their eyes are still fixed on me and I'm utterly positive we'll be spending every upcoming Friday night this way.

It's hard to imagine Oprah saying this but I add, "Are you ready for your first dungeon crawl?"

They're not just ready, they're enraptured!

"What the hell is on your chin?" Subject D asks.

The rapt spell has been broken as they all clamor to guess what is on my chin.

"I think you got a zit right before my eyes."

"I think it's a tomato."

"I think it's hypnotizing us into playing DUNGEONS & DRAGONS instead of watching Sex and the City reruns and eating hot chocolate exploding cake."

It's not a zit or a tomato or any kind of cool hypnotic infrared device I've built into my chin. It was a piece of cocktail napkin and enough to keep them quiet long enough to set the scene. I highly recommend that all new Dungeon Masters tape something red to your chins. Works like a charm.

"So we're going in the dungeon?" Subject C asks. "Are we dressed appropriately for that?"

DRESS FOR SUCCESS!

Seasons change, but these wardrobe essentials remain timeless. Enhance your attire with the following pieces:

Boots of Teleportation: Teleport from anywhere to anywhere three times a day! Great when you're stuck in traffic, in a boring meeting, or on a bad date.

Celestial Armor: Lightweight and flattering on any figure! Perfect for layering!

Friend Shield Ring: The alternative to the junior high BFF charms! Command your band to keep your buddy safe when you're not around. She'll probably have to return the favor sometime.

Heward's Handy Haversack: Perfect party pouch! Pack it in—it never gets full. And your car keys and cell phone will always be on top!

Breastplate of Command: Command attention in this scene stealing get-up! Your aura will not be ignored.

Bracelet of Friends: What's more fun than jug full of Jell-O shots? Sharing them with your buddies, of course. Call on your favorite four anytime, anywhere with this nifty charm bracelet.

"You're an experienced adventurer," I answer. "You're always dressed appropriately."

"How do you dress appropriately for a dungeon—oh, never mind."

"Eberk is about fourteen thousand years old. He's way too old for that kind of lifestyle."

"Not Regdar," Subject A says. "Look at him. He's the kind of guy who keeps his bondage gear in a shoebox under his bed and busts it out on the third date. And just as you're thinking you've finally found a normal-ish guy, he'll ask you to please put on the master's mask and hog tie him in the living room."

Poor Regdar! What would the guys in R&D think? "It's not that kind of dungeon," I explain. "It's a dungeon where monsters live. Get your minds out of Mr. Bunky's Quality Leather shop and back in the game."

They oblige, but I can see from the half-assed attempts to keep the smirks from their faces, the reprieve will be short-lived.

I continue. "On the side of a cliff, you find an entryway built into the stone." At this point, I am instructed to ask the group if any of them have a light source.

"Just my sparkling personality," Subject E answers.

"A flashlight?" Subject A asks. "I'd probably bring one of those into a dungeon."

I instruct them to read what is listed under weapons and read their special abilities on their character sheets.

"I can see in the dark!" Subject C shouts. "Everyone follow me."

"Sorry, Dopey," Subject E says. "You're following me. I have the highest initiative, remember?"

I'm so proud. My little manicured, designer-outfitted, socialite-in-training best friend just used the word "initiative" properly in a sentence. I move to her side of the table and kiss the top of her head. Oprah indeed!

Subject B looks over Subject A's shoulder and notices Regdar the love slave is packing. Ten torches, that is. Inspired, Subject A sneaks a peak at Subject E's equipment and calls Lidda out on keeping her torches hush hush too.

"If I'm going down, you're coming with me," she tells her friend. No matter how far removed you are from reality, a little bit of your true self still manages to make its way onto the play mat.

"You guys are selfish," Subject C says. "I'm an old man. You were going to make me strain my ancient eyes in the dark because you didn't want to use up your light stash."

Subject B grabs Lidda's character sheet. "What else have you got in there? A case of Lizard-Be-Gone?"

Subject E genuinely feels bad. She would absolutely share her torches with any of us in real life. "I didn't know how to read my character sheet. It's not my fault."

"Okay, so it's my fault," I say. "I'm a bad teacher. But I'm a fine baker and if you hurry up and play nice you will see for yourselves."

They regroup and regain what little focus they had before the Great Light Debate and I continue with the adventure.

"The entry way is cluttered but otherwise empty. At the end of the entryway you see double doors leading farther into the cliff. The heavy wooden doors are shut tight. What do you want to do?"

"We came this far," Subject B says. "Might as well keep going."

They agree and I ask them how they plan to get through the doors.

Subject A moves Regdar into room 2. "Uh, walk in?"

"You can't just walk in," I say. "The door is locked."

"So I opened it," she explains, matter of fact.

Subject A and Subject C appear to agree with her logic because they follow suit.

"Hey!" Subject B shouts. "Can they just ride my coattails like that?"

"Of course they can. You're supposed to be working together. But you can't just walk through the door. You can kick it down or pick the lock or put your ear to it and see if you hear anything on the other side."

"Let's kick it!" Subject A says.

"Just so I don't get yelled at again," Subject E says, referring to her character sheet. "Lidda apparently has the ability to pick a lock. Should I try?"

"Let's kick it!" Subject A says again.

The group seems to agree. Oh, good. Finally some dice rolling going on. "If you're going to kick it down, you need to roll the twenty-sided die and add that number to your Strength modifer."

Subject E is disappointed. "There's math involved?"

Subject A rolls an eighteen and adds her Strength score of three for a total of twenty-one. She succeeds.

"Oh my God, I'm so awesome!"

"You mean Regdar is awesome," Subject D corrects.

"I *am* Regdar," she answers, mashing her fists in the air. I picture her later tonight kicking in the front door of her craftsman-style home where her husband and baby are asleep and announcing, "Honey, I'm home!" I might have created a monster, or in this case, a fighter.

"You want a piece of me?" she asks everyone at the table.

Starting to realize what the character sheet has to offer, the rest of the group looks over their ability scores, comparing them to one another. I'm hoping this will teach them that every character has something unique to offer the party, whether it's Strength or Charisma or skills. Instead it turns into sixth grade.

"I'm stronger than you," Eberk says to Lidda.

"I'm prettier than you," Lidda says to Eberk.

"Pretty isn't an ability," Subject C says. "Is it?"

"Not in this game," I say.

"Well, then I'm smarter," she says. "Lidda is the whole package."

"Can I kill her?" Subject C asks.

. . . .

"Stop it!" I say. My dreams of Oprah are starting to turn into Jerry Springer. "This is *Dungeons & Dragons*. Not Resentments and Grudges. You're a team. Together you're the whole package."

Excellent. Oprah's back in the house. I think even she would appreciate the sentiment, since it's apparently true with every group of friends—minis and life size.

The girls drop the personality competition and trip down bad memory lane to return to kicking tiny lizard butt.

"Regdar has succeeded in kicking down the door. *(Cue erupting cheer)* But the noise has awakened the kobolds. They're just inside and they look pissed."*(Cue ooooohs.)*

"Where are the dragons? " Subject C asks.

"There are no dragons in this adventure."

"How can this be called *Dungeons & Dragons* if we're in a dungeon with no dragons?"

"That's false advertising," Subject D claims.

"Sometimes there are dragons, but not in this particular adventure."

"I'd kind of like to see a dragon," Subject C says, sounding so sincere I wish I could conjure one up for her to take home.

"Maybe next time," I say, and to my surprise she says okay.

"So about these kobolds," I say, guiding us back to the adventure at hand. "What do you want to do about them?"

"Kill them?" Subject A asks.

"You can try."

"I'm sorry," Subject E says. "I'm just not feeling the whole lizard thing. All I can think of Magnum, the iguana my brother had when he was fourteen. He was kind of cute. It feels wrong to kill him."

I hold the kobold mini under her nose. "These aren't Magnum. They're not on sale in some mall pet store. They are very evil reptilian beasts and they probably want to kill you."

"Still not feeling it," she says.

"I'd really like a dragon," Subject C says again.

"We couldn't kill a dragon either," Subject B comments. "They're probably on the endangered species list and we'd go to jail for as much as stepping on its toe."

Admittedly the kobolds aren't getting my sweat glands pumping either, especially considering some of the beasts Teddy has thrown at us. I have yet to encounter a dragon in game play, but I'm willing to compromise to keep the girls happy.

"I can't give you a dragon but I'll give you a vampire. Poof! The lizards have morphed into the evil and powerful Count—Evil Pants." I'm winging it, remember? Give me a break.

Subject D comes to the rescue. I think. "Count Cameltoe?"

"Ew!" the girls squeal. We've regressed from sixth grade to second grade. *Next floor, kindergarten!*

"You said evil pants and that's the first thing that came to mind."

"Now it's on," Subject E says. "Let's rid the world of cameltoe for good!"

Lidda capitalizes on having the highest initiative and makes the first move. "I take out my short bow and nail him straight through the heart. He falls dead."

"You don't get to determine if he falls dead," I say. "That's where I come in. And you don't even know if you've hit yet. Roll the appropriate die to see what happens."

Disappointed but determined, she rolls d20 and adds four as instructed by her character sheet. "Twenty-one! I win!"

"Wrong game," I say, "But yes, you definitely hit. Now roll for damage."

She rolls a two on the d4. "He feels it, but it's not nearly enough to kill him." I say.

Subject C is pensive. "He's a vampire, right? So we need a cross or garlic or sunlight. Throw a torch at him."

"We aren't equipped with garlic," Subject B says regarding Aramil. "But we do have the second-highest initiative so we go next, right?"

Gold star for Subject B. It took me at least three games to figure out what Teddy meant when he said to roll for initiative. I can feel the beams of pride radiating from my face. Or maybe that's sugar and oil oozing from my pores from thirteen mini cupcakes. Subject B and D confer and decide to try out Aramil's magical bag of tricks rather than use his longsword.

"We're taking the bastard down with a *magic missile*," Subject D announces like she's on a game show. *We'll take magic missile for the block, please.*

Magic missile is guaranteed to hit so the only roll of the die needed is to determine damage. They roll a total of three. It's enough to take down a kobold but seeing as how I've replaced the cold blooded with the blood sucking, I have no idea how many hit points a vampire can take. Probably more than five and they seem to be just starting to enjoy themselves, so I keep Count Cameltoe alive.

"He's hurting but he's still alive," I tell them.

Before Subject A can send Regdar into battle, she makes a confession.

"I've always kind of harbored a secret fantasy about vampires. I can't help it. Ever since I saw *The Lost Boys*, I think they're kind of sexy."

They're a chorus of oohs and ahhs and me too's. Yet again Kiefer Sutherland's hotness interrupts another D&D game. As it turns out, *The Lost Boys* affected us all.

"I'm kind of picturing Kiefer Sutherland's vampire, and hitting him with my greatsword isn't really the first thing that comes to mind."

I guess we are playing a fantasy game, but I'm not sure I want to be at the helm when Subject A plays out her fancy with an undead, fang-ridden Kiefer.

Subject E adds her two cents. "I'm definitely getting a hottie vibe from the Count as well, but in a dirty, throw-you-against-the-wall type of way."

"Ooh, like Tommy Lee!" Subject B says, clapping her hands. "So hot!"

My little Christmas card crafting friend is clap-happy over Tommy Lee?

"Let's not kill him," Subject D says. "Let's wound him enough to make him amenable to being our slave."

"Yes! He can take me to my cousin's wedding. Please. I can't bear the thought of wrestling the flower girls for the bouquet. They're small but they're wily."

Watch out, there's a major tangent heading our way and like a magic carpet my friends are about to get on it and ride away.

"Look," Subject A begins. "I'm not against finishing this game, or even playing again sometime, but if I don't get my hands on some chocolate in the next twelve seconds, I'm going to bite the heads of these miniature people and spit them machine-gun style in your face."

Yikes! Cameltoe, Kiefer Sutherland, vampiric fantasies, and six molten volcano cakes sitting on the counter. How can I compete? I give in.

As they plunge into their chocolate volcanoes, I feel like the mood in here is on fast forward. My friends are chattering incessantly, their cheeks are flushed, and their eyes are blurring from laughing. Subject B is fanning herself in attempt to cool off from a long, arduous battle. Or perhaps she's still thinking of Tommy Lee. And it may have been the alcohol or the sugar high or me projecting my feelings onto the girls, but I dare say they wouldn't be averse to trying this again sometime.

"What do you think my husband would say I if I told him I won't be home on Friday nights because I joined a D&D game?"

Subject B is all over it. "No one has to know if we're actually playing. It would be nice to have a night away."

"Maybe we could rotate houses," Subject E says.

"And games," Subject D adds, looking sideways at me. "D&D at your house. Texas Hold 'em at my house."

"Deal," I say. As long as softball isn't at anyone's house.

10 MONSTERS WOMEN ENCOUNTER EVERY DAY

The world of _Dungeons & Dragons_ is chock full of evil monsters, and guess what? So is the world you live in. Malevolent monster or toxic friend? Chances are you've already come face to face with the following beasts.

Joystealer: Who hasn't encountered a joystealer once or twice? In fact, you probably befriended her, bought her great birthday presents, invited her to dinner, and lent her your favorite cashmere wrap. And what did you get in return? A toxic friend who feeds off of your fear, passions, joys, and boyfriends. She'll drain the life out you and then return your cashmere wrap with a big old ketchup stain on it.

Berserker: Berserkers come in all forms in the D&D world. In our world they probably take the shape of a sports fan, road rager, or new boyfriend's ex-girlfriend. Berserkers seek attention, victory, and fame and will trample anything or anyone in their path to get it. While amusing to be around when they're working themselves into a frenzy, if they direct that energy in your direction—duck.

Deathdrinker: Another toxic friend. Here's the tag-along who feeds off your misery. They're seldom around to celebrate your successes but they're the first ones to call to say, "So sorry to hear about. . . ." Don't fall for it. Misery loves company and deathdrinkers are the first ones to crash the party. Go do a good deed and really piss them off.

Howler Wasp Queen: Two, four, six, eight, who do we love to hate? Yep, it's the howler wasp queen in all her prom-queenie glory. What is it about her that makes her male counterparts glom around her like a colony of lovesick twelve-year-olds at a Hilary Duff concert? Can't you just see her? Button nose, headband, navy blue sweater around her shoulders. Howler wasps have one agenda when it comes to their stinging attacks—proximity. How superficial is that? If you're going to hate on someone, at least have a better reason than "because they're there." How about because she's a vapid, venomous, bullying monster.

Troll: Of course the evil troll would make the list. Isn't that what you and your friends call the evil ex, the meddling mother-in-law, the cardio addict at the gym who pops nary a bead of sweat after two hours on the treadmill? Yep, all trolls, but not the kind you'll encounter in _Dungeons & Dragons_. Watch out for the book bag-brandishing bully trolls who inhabit playgrounds. They may look innocent—cute even—with their pigtails and turtlenecks decorated with hearts and whales, but they're just as deadly as their grown-up counterparts.

Justice Archon: Do any of your friends believe they were super heroes in a past life? If so, you probably know a justice archon or two. Like the name implies, these righteous dudes are quick to sniff out evil and become incensed by the odor. They can turn a perfectly good dinner party debate into a civil war before the last aperitif has been swallowed. Debauched in the living room! Decent in the dining room! You may not think it's a big deal if the grocery checker thought your honey crisps were the less expensive red delicious types, but if it were up to the justice archon, you'd be sent to hell in a hand basket full of ripped-off apples.

Plague Walker: Cough, cough, sniffle, sniffle, look who's popping penicillin again. The stinkin' plague walkers are a flytrap for germs and for some odd reason, they're damn proud of it. If it's not a sinus, ear, or urinary tract infection, it's Seasonal Affective Disorder, arthritis, and early stage Alzheimer's. Too bad they're never too sick to decline an invitation to show up and bore your friends with what ails them this week. The good news is the only thing they're generally full of is crap, and you can't catch that.

Corruptor of Fate: Not only do you know this creature, you've probably played the part. The corruptor of fate is by far the most evil monster a man can encounter when he's trying to get with a girl. All that money spent on drinks, all the time wasted hearing about your pet hamster, all those faux compliments, all for what? Nothing thanks to your girlfriend, who has shifted into the corruptor and refuses to leave the two of you alone. You may not be able to control fate, but you can corrupt it. How's that for a buzz kill?

Defacer: The defacer is pretty darn scary in the D&D world. They appear from below to strike their prey, stun the living daylights out of it, and then go in for the kill. Why? So they can steal your face, of course! A defacer in real life is even scarier. Know that friend who compliments your sweater, then shows up two days later wearing it? Soon enough she's got the same boots as you and wears the same nostalgic shade of green eye shadow that compliments the long shag 'do you've been sporting for months now. Imitation is not the sincerest form of flattery. It's the quickest way to an ass kicking.

Whisper Demon: Remember that classic (and yes, I'm using the word classic loosely) Melissa Manchester song "You Should Hear How She Talks About You?" The whisper demon does, and she's hissing all the dirty details in your ears. Try to block it out because it will make you crazy. The whisper demon goes above and beyond typical lunchtime gossip. She wants to see you flush with rage. She wants to beat you down. In D&D, a whisper demon's ghoulish whispers drive their prey batty. In real life, these beasts will certainly drive you insane if you let them. Try humming a classic Melissa Manchester song instead. It may not block them out, but it will scare them quite a bit.

Death Becomes Her

I was the first to arrive the next Monday for our game. Teddy hadn't even unfurled the play mat before my books, sharpened pencils, and mismatched dice were sitting posture perfect at the conference room table. Perhaps my foray into Dungeon Mastering has made me more respectful of my own Dungeon Master. It's not an easy feat to bring new players into the game and somehow keep them interested enough to continue coming back.

It's not long before the rest of the group shows up and we take our required half hour to catch up on all the stuff we didn't catch up on during the previous seven-and-a-half hours we spent together at work. Teddy draws a map on the play mat and tells us to gather our minis at the city center. Our characters leveled up recently, and I can't help but feel a little bit proud of Astrid and her friends. If I had a video camera, I'd be recording her as she takes her first steps onto the play mat as a 5th-level sorcerer. As we continue to play, we gain experience not just in points, but also in knowledge, which makes our campaigns move quicker and challenges harder.

Today we're picking up from last week's ugly battle. We're on the hunt for a lost schema, which for anyone who doesn't watch *24* is a diagram or a plan showing the basic outline for something. If we recover it, our benefactor Lady Elaydren will reward us handsomely. This chick keeps popping up in our adventurers. She's a *nonplayer character,* a character played by the DM and someone we encounter along the way. Personally, I think Lady Elaydren is a high-maintenance pain in the ass. She's already sent us on some wild chases for crap she's either misplaced or carelessly left around so it could be stolen. She's apparently got enough gold pieces in her bank account to pay people to clean up her messes, but if it were up to me I'd tell her to spend some coin and get a clue. This co-dependent, poor-me victim routine is getting old.

Finding the schema was easy enough. Getting it back safely is proving to be a different story. It's taking its toll on our characters, too. We're a little worse for the wear after having survived a swarm of beetles and a nasty gaggle of rats. Even Astrid took a few hits from the horrid rodents that were attracted not just to beauty but also to the weakest-looking player in the bunch. It's a strategy equivalent to sucker punching an oblivious pedestrian in the back of the neck. Of my thirteen hit points, I'm down to seven and I've used almost all of my daily allotment of spells. Provided we have a break in the action, Amok can put us back together again. But judging from the sparkle behind Teddy's scratch-resistant lenses, he's got a few more tricks up his sleeves.

We find ourselves in what appears to be the remains of a temple.

"You notice the temple has a quiet, peaceful feeling about it," Teddy says, and immediately everyone is suspicious.

"I've got a bad feeling about this place."

"Teddy just said it was calm and serene. Let's pretend we're at Canyon Ranch."

"It's the calm before the storm," Hank says.

"We should take a quick look around," Helena says, or rather demands. "If nothing looks out of the ordinary we can stop and rest. Otherwise at least we'll be prepared."

"You go first," I say. If we have to sacrifice someone to the temple of doom, it might as well be the slaphappy monk.

The list of skills your character can master might seem endless and impossible to choose from, but it's always better to be a master of a few than mediocre at a lot. Of course your class plays into your choices, but like a karaoke machine and an open bar, the following skills are a great addition to any party: Spot, Listen, Search, Concentration, Diplomacy, and Gather Information.

"Or you could go first and cast *detect magic*," she offers. "You do know that spell, don't you?" She says this like she's asking if I know the difference between white and winter white.

"Of course I do!" I say. Normally I'd bust out the old *detect magic* machine but I've only got two 0-level spells left and I'd like to keep an *acid splash* or a *ray of frost* handy in case those pesky beetles return.

"What's the point of playing a sorcerer if you aren't going to cast spells?" Helena asks, which is a totally stupid question. Just because you have a thousand dollars in the bank doesn't mean you have to spend it all. Seriously. It doesn't. Plus, my frugality might actually benefit my group later on.

I look to Teddy, who has had to referee a few outbursts on more than one occasion. "I'd like to cast *shut up* on Tenoctris."

"That's not a spell, Astrid," Teddy says, rooting through his bag for his Tom Clancy novel.

"How about *fat lip*?"

"You don't want to go fist-to-fist with me," she says, and she's probably right so I pretend I don't hear her.

"I thought monks were supposed to be quiet," I say instead. "Why don't you go bake some bread or save a village full of children?"

"Why don't you summon a pumice stone and give yourself a pedicure?" she says.

Note to self: Lay off the peep-toe shoes until I can get an appointment. And how the heck does this girl know what a pumice stone is?

"No one needs to detect anything," Armando says. "Jak will go first. If anyone wants to join him, please do."

Jak is almost always volunteering for the jobs no one wants in an attempt to make us forget he's the guy who tumbled out of a horse-drawn carriage into a drainage ditch and lost himself two hit points from sitting on his short sword. I'm willing to forget as long as Jak's got my back. Keeping history in mind, that may or may not be a good thing.

Ursula agrees to join Jak, and if she goes we all go because no one likes to be left alone without our resident fighter. I ain't happy about it, but my only other choice is to hang back in the creepy but calm temple and give myself a pedicure. Dad would be disappointed, but in this case, I follow the crowd.

We move from the entry into a room Teddy has marked out in black marker on the mat. There are piles of rubble and columns of stone, but otherwise nothing of any interest.

Hank is suspicious. "There's got to be more here. Yakama would like to look around some more."

"Give me a Spot check," Teddy says, prompting Hank to roll the twenty-sided die. He's got a decent amount of points next to "Spot" under skills, so he notices two passageways that presumably lead to other parts of the temple and our probable death. I can feel Astrid getting weaker by the millisecond.

"Let's go," Tenoctris says, and she's not talking about *out of here*. "We should keep exploring. At least find a safe place to spend the night."

"Like maybe a Days Inn?" I ask. "What's wrong with right here?"

"We still don't know where we are," Ursula explains. "And we have to return the schema safely."

Drat! The cursed schema. If it was so important, why didn't Lady Elaydren keep it in a high security bank vault or a tripped-out panic room built specially for her castle?

"Is it me, or does anyone else picture Lady Elaydren looking like Joan Collins?"

No one has time to answer before Teddy plops a giant tank of a creature smack in the middle of our path.

"Holy hell," Armando says. "We're so dead."

"What is that thing?" Hank asks. It stands at least three times our minis' heights and resembles a toaster with beady green eyes and fists fitted with axe blades. Actually it looks nothing like a toaster, but it does look like something that could toast us.

"Astrid wants to go now," I say.

"We haven't rolled for initiative yet," Helena says.

"Not *go* as in *my turn*. Go as in *beat it the hell out of here*."

"Is that a warforged?" Lucy asks. Teddy doesn't answer her so she asks again as Ursula. Teddy confirms.

Whatever it is, it fights dirty. No sooner have we caught our breath than it fires a flaming crossbow bolt at us before ducking under cover. A second flaming bolt goes whizzing by.

Teddy shifts into narrator mode. "After near misses with the flaming bolts you hear a booming voice call, 'Weak flesh! You are face-to-face with Saber, the greatest of the devoted followers of the Lord of Blades. Throw down the schema and walk away. This day does not have to end with blood on my hands.'"

Well, thank goodness for that!

"Who's got the schema?" Ursula asks.

If it had been in my backpack, it'd already be in Mr. Saber's hot little hands and I'd be halfway through a pint of mead at the Broken Anvil, warning fellow patrons to stay away from that useless Lady Elaydren and her tired bag of damsel-in-distress tricks.

"I've got the schema," Jak says.

"Try to stay covered," Yakama commands. "Do what you have to protect it."

What? Are these people crazy? Protect the schema and put us in harm's way? Astrid's life is worth more than Lady Elaydren's hefty ransom.

"My friend lives in New York City," I say. "She carries cash around for the sole purpose of giving it to muggers. They're much more inclined to leave you unharmed in exchange for twenty bucks. I'm sure Mr. Saber would do the same."

"Everybody roll for initiative," Teddy says. I don't need a roll of the die to tell me I'm seriously losing this battle.

Jak goes first and uses his action to move himself to a safer spot behind a column. Ursula is next and she attacks the beast with a throwing axe. She hits, but it's not enough to do much damage. He's made of freakin' stone and steel after all.

Amok and Yakama are next and use their longbows. Their arrows barely put a dent in the beast's hide.

"Astrid," Teddy says. "It's your turn."

Out of the six 1st-level spells I can use a day, I've only got two left. I cast *magic missile* and bring my total down to one—the fewest I've ever had.

"Puem! Puem!" I say. I hit but again, do little damage.

No one is eager to get to close to this guy. Except Tenoctris, who apparently believes that showing off is as worthy an ability as making your own piecrust or folding a cloth napkin into the shape of a swan.

"I don't have a choice," she says. "The only weapons I have are my fists."

Suddenly I feel like I'm in a Steven Seagal movie. What is wrong with this girl?

Helena moves her mini the allotted spaces for her turn and gets up close and personal with Saber. She taps into her inner barbarian and lands a few healthy punches. All it seems to do is piss him off and put her in close range to his flaming bolts.

"Tenoctris doesn't get out of the way quick enough and gets an arrow to her back," Teddy says. "She takes thirteen points of damage."

There's a collective gasp around the table. She was already beaten up pretty badly from getting into the faces of various monsters. Can someone get her a long-range weapon? Last week's session caused her to lose twenty-six of her forty-one hit points, and losing thirteen more points brings her total down to . . . two! Ouch!

"She's almost dead!" Lucy says. "We need to get her out of his range!"

Jak is next, but everyone urges him to stay behind the column and use a long-range weapon. He's got the stupid schema, after all.

"Why don't we trade the schema for Tenoctris?" I ask out of character. More than saving Tenoctris's life, I'd like to stick it to Lady Elaydren by showing up empty-handed.

"I have hit points to spare," Ursula says. "I'll get up there and hit him with my greatsword. Maybe he'll take his aggression out on me."

Jak apparently knows a thing or two about warforged creatures. "They like to fight to the death—finish what they started."

That doesn't bode entirely well for Tenoctris, who's just about done for. Still, Amok and Yakama take turns throwing themselves in harm's way, attempting to distract the warforged from the easy target squirming at his feet. They both hit, but little damage appears to be done.

"Okay, Astrid," Teddy says, and again, he sounds sorry that it's my turn. "What do you want to do?"

What do I want to do? I want to run screaming from this beast-infested temple to the nearest bar and knock back a few pints. Or make myself invisible and shove my fingers in my ears and stick my tongue out at the warforged and use my turn to dance around MC Hammer-style singing *Can't Touch This.* I've got one 1st-level spell left, which could be *magic missile* or a *ray of enfeeblement* or some other spell that would prove useless against this monster. I could wrap myself in *mage armor* to offer Astrid a little extra protection, which might be the smartest option. I could use one of my two 0-level spells remaining, like *acid splash, disrupt undead* or *ray of frost.* Even I know hitting this creature with any of them would be as practical as eating an entire cheesecake while walking on a treadmill. I'm about to say screw it and send off the last of my *magic missiles* when I think about Tenoctris, lying face down on the ground with a flaming arrow in her back. I glance at Helena, who is looking at her mini and probably wondering when she'll have time to roll-up another character after Tenoctris bites it next round. I wonder if she's disappointed. Maybe she really likes Tenoctris. Maybe she feels the protective tug at her heart looking at her little girl laying facedown on the play mat with her face full of marker ink. Why did she name her Tenoctris anyway? Sensing me watching her, Helena looks up and catches my gaze. My turn is the only thing that stands between her and impending death. She half shrugs, almost like she's giving me permission to save myself. *Just get it over with*, I see in her eyes.

"I'd like to cast *mage armor*," I say. "On Tenoctris."

"Oh, good!" Lucy says clapping her hands and regressing to her mommy-mode. "We can save her!"

"It's a touch spell," Teddy explains. "You'll actually have to move to where she is to cast it."

"I know," I say. "I can do it." Fortunately I can move enough spaces on my turn to touch Tenoctris and encase her in a force field. I'll be close but at least not in direct contact with the beast.

Mage armor

On Saber's turn, his flaming bolt bounces off Tenoctris, thanks to the *mage armor*. His attention is diverted between the five of us, but even with my spells depleted and teammates weakened, we manage to take the sucker down. Lady Elaydren gets her schema, we get our gold pieces. Astrid invests in a cool new accessory—*Heward's handy haversack*—a magical backpack that never weighs more than five pounds no matter how much you over pack. As a bonus, whatever you're looking for will always be right on top. Oprah would rank this number one on her list of favorite things for sure. And oh, yes, I almost forgot. Tenoctris survived unscathed and unchanged. Or so I thought.

A couple days later I was deeply absorbed in putting together a Power Point presentation when Helena showed up in my cubicle.

"I figured if you were going to keep playing DUNGEONS & DRAGONS, you might need these," she said, dropping a bundle on my desk and leaving.

"Thanks," I muttered, figuring it was a list of other groups in search of members. Wrong. Inside the velvet satchel was a complete set of my very own matching dice. And they were the pinkest pink I've seen since Butch Cut Barbie's corvette.

No need to write which die to roll on your palm. Write your own Cliff Notes and tuck them into your dice bag. It's much more acceptable than asking every turn, "Wait. What does rolling for initiative mean?"

Love is in the Air

My boyfriend had been begging me to try it. What would my friends think of me if they knew? What would my mother think? Oh, God! Apparently it's something lots of couples do, but no one I know. Or maybe women do it but they don't talk about it.

—Jodi, New York

I resisted at first thinking I wasn't that kind of girl, not to mention I would have to endure hours and hours of pain-filled so-called entertainment. But on his birthday I caved, wanting to give him something memorable. I showed up at his apartment in a chainmail bikini and bag of dice and said okay, just this one time.

—Kristina, New Jersey

From what I heard it was really hard and could take hours to figure out. Who has that kind of time? I mean, you can't just whip it out and go at it on an airplane. Sometimes a quickie like Crazy 8's is all you need for a good time.

—Roxy, Washington

I admit, I was curious but I still wasn't willing to try it. I like the fact that you have to do it as a group because I'm a very extroverted and kind of an exhibitionist. My biggest fear was that I would actually enjoy it and want to do it all the time. I do have to work, you know.

—Desiree, New Mexico

What? Huh? Of course, we're still talking about D&D, pervette. What did you think? What kind of book with *Girl's* in the title would be complete without the obligatory section on meeting a potential mate? Sorry, ladies, I know most of you are self-sufficient women of the new millennium who *don't need no stinkin' man* (to quote Subject D) but for the few of us—I mean you—who might not be, read on.

Think about it: The odds are in your favor. D&D is a world populated mostly by men. It's like Alaska, only without the long flight to the middle of nowhere and lack of daylight.

This thought didn't cross my mind at first. I was playing with co-workers and if I wanted to hit on them, I would have gotten drunk at the holiday party years ago and karaoked some Journey tunes to them. It did occur to my mother, whose minimal knowledge of D&D consisted of 1) Boys play it and 2) Weird boys play it. Apparently a weird prospective son-in-law is better than no son-in-law.

I put on my best CNN journalist face (okay, it's more *Access Hollywood*) and did a little investigating. I asked several women who have been playing D&D for years and found nothing surprising. They all either got into the game because a boyfriend or husband was playing it, or came into a group via purely platonic means and ended up meeting their knight in masterwork armor. You know how some men think it's cool when women swear at the television during a football game (and not in a "get this crap off my TV and go mow the lawn" sort of way)? Well, some men think women roleplayers are pretty chill too. What guy wouldn't dig a chick who can get down and dirty in a dungeon? Not many guys would deny a chance to tutor the woman of his dreams on the fine art of flanking or how to select the proper skill set for a changeling rogue. My friend who shall remain nameless because no one knows we're friends said, "A woman who plays D&D is hot. No question about it. She could have warts and bad breath, but tell me she's a 9th-level halfling rogue and I'm pretty much sold." I should have prefaced that by saying his last girlfriend won him over by burping her phone number to him at a baseball game.

Probably the biggest nugget of proof floating around in the pudding is the reaction some roleplaying women have to newbie women invading their game group. One respondent I investigated gave a rather snarky response.

"Why are you writing this? I don't want more women to start playing. I like being the only woman at the table."

Ah! Of course! Who wouldn't like being the only wench among warriors? The alpha female mentality exists almost everywhere women do and a D&D game is no exception. Experienced women can feel resentful when a new player joins the group. Suddenly all eyes are on her, helping her decipher the difference between a d20 and a d10 and showing her where to find the initiative modifier on her character sheet. Sorry, ladies, your little secret is out. Not only is a game of D&D a good time, it's a good time to meet new people. But remember, if you're among the "new people." Be respectful of those who came before you, don't let your only motivation for playing be to score a date with the Dungeon Master, and don't forget the "no flirting" rule. Know your boundaries. If flirting seems okay in character, go for it, but keep in mind scoring the Dungeon Master's digits is secondary to playing the game.

Now if you'll excuse me, I have to reapply my mascara, paint my nails, and pluck my eyebrows. My game is starting in fifteen minutes.

Dear Diary,

All this chasing down that kooky Lady Elaydren's lost items is really wearing on my nerves. I don't know why we have to drop everything when she comes calling. Sure, the pay is great, but I'd almost take a job bussing tables at Ye Old Mead and Ale Factory rather than find myself in the bowels of some dirty dungeon shaking in my brand new boots after coming face to face with a raging, pissed off warforged. Almost.

Anyway, I was in desperate need of a little R&R. What better way to unwind than to have a party? Amok told me it is a human custom to get together once a week for what they call a game night. That's a rather charming idea from such an unrefined race. So the date was set, directions were given, and my friends agreed to come. Even though my elven friends and I normally find dwarves to be a bit—how shall I say—boorish, Ursula is a rare exception. I gratefully count her among my best friends. Unfortunately, the same can't be true of her friends. They don't take up much room vertically, not like a human does, but they're so broad and compact only a few can hang out in the kitchen before you feel totally claustrophobic. And they had no regard for the effort that went into planning my menu. Once they found out there was pilsner in the gouda-gruyere fondue, they were passing the pot around and drinking straight from it like it was champagne pouring from some silly sports championship trophy. How rude! Humans may not know what fork to use half the time, but at least they know how to properly dunk (no double dipping) into a pot of steaming fondue. The only good thing about the height of dwarves is that they're so short you can pass appetizers over their uncouth little heads without them even noticing.

In addition to the ill-fated fondue, I served mini quiches with baby shrimp and artichokes, gorgonzola and cranberry tarts wrapped in a salted butter filo crust, handmade lobster and asparagus ravioli in a creamy garlic butter and wine sauce, escarole with roasted shallots, flamenco potato salad with lemon-dill dressing, arugula salad with goat's milk yogurt dressing, chick pea fritters, and for dessert a lovely fresh lime mousse and lemon-buttermilk pound cake with fresh berries. If I'd had more time I would have come up with something more elaborate.

Everyone was having a fine time listening to music, eating my delicious treats, and watching the humans make asses of themselves on the dance floor. (Seriously, do they really have no idea how silly their faces look? What's with the eyes half closed? Are they mesmerized by the shuffling sounds of their feet?) A fine time, until Tenoctris the uninvited showed up.

What the hell? I was very careful not to mention my soiree around her. I didn't even send paper invitations lest one fall out of someone's backpack. But sure enough, there she was in all her peasant, barefoot glory. She was sophisticated enough to bring a bottle of wine. She probably squashed the grapes herself with those boney little shifter feet of hers. I think I'll donate it to the half-elves, thank you. She got her grubby little mitts all over the appetizer trays and stuffed her face full of my culinary delights! My delights! She claimed she just came from jiu-jitsu class and was ravenous. Ursula reminded me that her raging metabolism and calloused fingers could very well save my butt one of these days. Whatever.

Amok taught everyone how to play a human game called charades. It was great fun, especially considering that half of the guests were so toasted they couldn't find a clue with a big red X and a pickaxe, let alone act one out. That was pretty fun. Not like pass-the-gnome fun, but still amusing nonetheless. It was all fun and games until someone (okay, me) got caught up in a dare and let a fireball rip through my neighbor's yard. I just learned the spell and quite honestly can't get enough of it. It's an amazing ball of fire shooting from my fingertip! Fortunately, a clothesline and a rose bush took the brunt of the damage. I need to remember to invite my neighbor next time.

The fireball inspired us to have a bonfire in the clearing of the forest It was a beautiful night for a walk. Beautiful if you had remembered to bring your shoes, of course! Tenoctris looked sad at the prospect of having to walk several miles on feet that were already bruised and sore, not to mention unprotected.

"I guess I'll just see you guys tomorrow," she said.

I'm not one to fall for this passive-aggressive crap. I knew she wanted to come with us. Maybe the girl was really trying to make some sort of effort to be social. Emphasis on the "effort" part Maybe it was the moonlight or the zombitinis or the sight and sound of all my friends making merry in my living room, but I offered to lend her a pair of shoes. I was going to bring them to consignment anyway. To my surprise, and I think hers as well, she actually looked pretty good with a little extra lift. They did wonders to accentuate her calf muscles. I told her as much, and I think I made her blush. Then again it could have been the wine. I'm pretty sure I saw the beginnings of a smile.

Again, I'm proven correct in my theory. All a woman really needs to be happy in life is a new pair of shoes.

I think I'll take a nap now.

Until next time.

Love, Astrid

THE GIRL'S GUIDE TO
DUNGEONS & DRAGONS DECREE

Hey, Sisterhood of the Well-Tailored Pants—
you ready to roll? Bring your A-game to the table by
raising your right hand and repeating these words.

Henceforth, I promise I will:

◆ Never borrow my friend's dice if I have chocolate
frosting, barbeque sauce, or any other sticky
substance on my fingertips.

◆ Never make fun of players who choose to use
sound effects when casting spells.

◆ Never take out my real-life vendettas on the
fictional characters in the game.

◆ Never ask the Dungeon Master more than three
times in a single encounter, "Where are we again?"

◆ Never forget how hard it is to roll up a character and
therefore protect my fellow adventurers whenever
possible.

◆ Never deliberately bite the ends of all the Twizzlers®
so I don't have to share.

◆ Never leave home without a pack of matches and a
PowerBar.®

◆ Never underestimate the power of a man in a well-
made Stormtrooper suit.

◆ Never use "go back to your dungeon and play with
your dragons" as an insult again.

Bag of Holding: Regardless of what is put in the bag, it weighs a fixed amount. Perfect for traveling!

APPENDIX

Cheaters Never (well, hardly ever) Win

Cheat sheets aren't allowed in high school math class, but D&D ain't algebra. In this chapter you'll find a sample character sheet and an easily digestible glossary. And you can write the answers to which dice to roll in blue ink all over the palm of your hand.

I'm not going to lie—there's a lot to learn, but you can take it in small doses. The good news is you only need to know the basics to start playing and the rest comes from experience.

Designing Women

Your character sheet is all about your character and the way it's designed should be all about you. Feel free to use a pre-designed character sheet designed for each of the character classes, found in either the *Player's Handbook* or online at **wizards.com/dnd**.

There's no wrong way to customize your character sheet. You can include as little or as much as you want to. For instance, in addition to character's race, class, height and weight, Calvin has a character sheet that includes "looks." According to Calvin, Amok is "hot." Whatever. Just make sure all the relevant information pertaining to your character is readily available to you. Below is an example of a character sheet I created for Astrid. Her hotness goes without saying.

From the Desk of:
Astrid Bellagio

* You'll want to use a pencil to fill out your character sheet.

Shelly	Sorcerer	5	Elf			
Player Name	**Class**	**Level**	**Race**			
Chaotic Good	134	Female	5'8"	120 lbs.	8	
Alignment	**Age**	**Gender**	**Height**	**Weight**	**Shoe Size**	

* Your Armor Class is the number that enemies need to hit you in combat
* Your base attack is the number you add to your d20 attack roll. As you level up, this number will increase.
* Hit points are how many points you have until your character dies. Make sure you have an eraser handy.
* Your initiative modifier is added to your d20 initiative roll.

AC Armor Class	13	HP Hit Points	13
Base Attack Bonus	+2	Initiative Modifier	+3

* You'll also want to write down relevant character information you need to reference quickly, like the languages you speak and your character's racial traits.

Languages known: Common, Elven, Draconic & Goblin

Racial Traits: Low light vision, immunity to sleep spells, +2 racial saving throw bonus against enchantment, proficiency with long/shortbows, rapiers, and longswords, and ability to detect secret doors!

* Fortitude saves measure your defense against physical harm like poison, disease, or immobility. The ability modifier is your Constitution modifier (see below).
* Reflex saves measure your ability to get the heck out of the way of trouble. The ability modifier is your Dexterity modifier (see below).
* Will saves measure your resistance to mental take-overs like charm spells and hypnosis. The ability modifier is your Wisdom modifier (see below).

Saving Throws	Total	Base Save	Ability Modifiers
Fortitude	+1	+1	0
Reflex	+4	+1	+3
Will	+6	+4	+2

Ability	Ability Score	Modifiers/ Bonus	Skills	Key Ability	Skill Modifier	Ability Modifier	Ranks
Strength	11	0	Appraise	Int	2	0	0
Dexterity	16	+3	Balance	Dex	3	+3	0
Constitution	10	0	Bluff	Cha	5	+3	2
Intelligence	15	+2	Climb	Str	0	0	0
Wisdom	14	+2	Concentration	Con	7	0	7
Charisma	17	+3	Craft (Alchemy)	Int	9	+2	7
			Disguise	Cha	3	+3	0
Gold Pieces	Experience Points		Escape Artist	Dex	3	+3	0
3,956	16,785		Forgery	Int	2	+2	0
			Gather Information	Cha	3	+3	0
			Hide	Dex	3	0	0
			Intimidate	Cha	3	0	0
			Knowledge (arcana)	Int	9	+2	7
			Listen	Wis	6	+2	4
			Move Silently	Dex	3	0	0
			Ride	Dex	3	0	0
			Search	Int	4	+2	2
			Sense Motive	Wis	3	+1	2
			Spellcraft	Int	9	+1	8

Every character has these abilities. You fill in the scores.

❋ Write in the skills your character has and the appropriate modifiers. As you gain new skills, write them in.

❋ We all know how important it is to balance your checkbook. Make sure you have somewhere to track your loot and experience points.

Weapon	Roll this for damage	Add this to damage roll	Range	Notes
Shortspear	1d6 (1 six-sided die)	+1	20 ft	
Light Crossbow	1d8 (1 eight-sided die)	+5	80 ft	

Ammunition:_____

* List your weapons of mass destruction and ammunition here. If only the United Nations made character sheets mandatory.
* It helps to keep track of what you need to roll to figure out damage.

My Wands and Staffs:
Wand or Staff   Reference page
Wand of mage hand   Player's Handbook p.249
Wand of magic missile   Player's Handbook p.251
                              (I won this sucker in a battle)

* This part will be customized depending on what kind of character you're playing. A fighter probably doesn't have a wand or a staff, but she might have a hefty collection of swords.

My Spell Book:

0-Level Spells/day **6**   Spells I Know **6**   Spells I've cast today

Spell	Page #	Notes
Acid Splash	196	damage = 1d3
Detect Magic	219	information increases the longer I study the area
Detect Poison	219	use on creature, object or area
Disrupt Undead	223	make ranged touch attack to hit. Damage = 1d6
Ray of Frost	269	Freeze, sucka! make ranged touch attack. Damage = 1d3
Read Magic	269	decipher magical inscriptions on objects
Touch of Fatigue	294	touch attack. Creature becomes immediately tired

＊ Again, this part will be customizable depending your character.
＊ Write down spells as you acquire them.
＊ It helps to write down page numbers and which dice to roll to put them into effect.

1st-Level Spells/day **6**   Spells I Know **4**   Spells I've cast today

Spell	Page #	Notes
Mage Armor	249	must touch target. Gives +4 armor bonus
Magic Missile	251	always hits! Damage = 1d4+1
Ray of Enfeeblement	269	ranged touch attack. Damage = 1d6+1 to strength

2nd-Level Spells/day **4**   Spells I Know **2**   Spells I've cast today

Spell	Page #	Notes
Resist Energy	272	Reduce damage from 1 of 5 energy types by 10
Scorching Ray	274	Fire! ranged touch attack. Damage = 4d6

Miscellaneous Gear:

Balenciaga clutch	Lantern
Balenciaga hobo	10 torches
Balenciaga wallet	Flint & steel
3 pairs of Jimmy Choo shoes	50 tindertwigs

Notes: Astrid is cool.

Word Up

If you're going to play it, you need to say it. Here's a quick recap of all the new words you'll be using to pepper your every-day conversations.

Ability: One of the six basic physical and mental aspects of a character or monster represented by a numerical value. Abilities include Strength, Dexterity, Constitution, Intelligence, Wisdom, and Charisma. *The wizard fell down the well because his Dexterity wasn't up to snuff.*

Ability Check: A roll of the twenty-sided die to determine the outcome related to a particular ability. The ability modifier is added to the die roll. *If you want to sweet talk a troll into giving you directions, you'll need to make a Charisma ability check.*

Adventure: The "story" the Dungeon Master runs for the player characters. *We had a blast playing today thanks to the amazing adventure our DM prepared for us.*

Alignment: Your character's stance in the conflict between good and evil. Player characters can be lawful good, lawful neutral, neutral good, neutral, chaotic good, or chaotic neutral. Villains and monsters are lawful evil, neutral evil, or chaotic evil. *There is no alignment in D&D that prohibits the use of prescription drugs to cure depression.*

Armor Class (AC): A number that represents your chances of dodging a hit during combat. *The dwarf fighter has the highest Armor Class so she can withstand some serious blows.*

Attack Roll: A roll of the die that determines if an attack hits. *I always forget what die to use for the attack roll to see how much damage my* magic missiles *cause (it's a d4).*

Buff: The use of magic to beef up your character or fellow player's potential. *I buffed myself up with* mage armor *because I'm pretty sure the ogre could kick my ass.*

Character Sheet: A reference tool housing all of your character's important information such as hit points, Armor Class, spells known, weapons owned, and so on. *I wish he had a character sheet in real life so I could see what skills he has.*

Check: A roll of the twenty-sided die to determine the success or failure of an action. *The Dungeon Master needs us to roll a Spot check to see if anyone notices the giant white gorilla in the room.*

Class: Your character's chosen career. There are eleven in the *Player's Handbook*: barbarian, bard, cleric, druid, fighter, monk, paladin, ranger, rogue, sorcerer, and wizard. *I have been told I lack couth and social grace, so the best class for me is a barbarian.*

Dungeon Master (DM): The man or woman who commands the D&D universe in which the characters exist. *Our Dungeon Master is not only a great story-teller, he's also very patient and tolerant of new players.*

Experience Points (XP): The measure of your character's success. Experience points are earned after you and your party overcomes challenges such as recovering a missing schema or defeating an angry band of trolls. *We got six hundred experience points for tracking down and recovering the schema.*

Hit: A successful attack as determined by the roll of a die. *Nice roll! A twenty-three totally hits.*

Hit Points: How much damage your character can take. When a character's hit points drop to 0, he falls to the ground, out of the battle but not dead. *Cover me! I only have three hit points left!*

Initiative: The technique that determines who goes first in combat. Each player rolls a twenty-sided die to determine the order of combat. The highest roll goes first. *When we're heading into battle, I pray for a low initiative roll so Astrid doesn't have to go first.*

Level: The measure or your character's advancement or the power of spells. Your level is comparable to the grade you are in school (if school went up to twentieth grade and beyond). *When my character levels up, she will learn three new spells.*

Masterwork: Extraordinarily well-designed accessories like armor or weapons. *The stitching on this masterwork Chanel bag is incomparable.*

Melee: Close range, often hand-to-hand combat. *The Socs and the Outsiders were in melee when they had the rumble that put Dallas in the hospital.*

Metagaming: A broad term usually used to define any strategy, action, or method used in a game that transcends a prescribed rule set, uses external factors to affect the game, or goes beyond the supposed limits or environment set by the game. *I admit to metagaming when I saw the DM cringe after I said I'd go down the tunnel alone.*

Mini: Short for miniature. Your mini represents you on the battle grid. *No, I do not think my mini looks like a stripper, thank you very much.*

Modifier: A bonus (or penalty) number given to your character depending on certain scores. *Astrid's high Charisma and Dexterity give her great modifiers to skills based on those abilities.*

Nonplayer Character (NPC): Any character controlled by the Dungeon Master. *Lady Elaydren is the most annoying nonplayer character our DM has ever brought to life.*

Race: Your character's species. *The best race to play if you want to live a long time is an elf.*

Player Character (PC): The character that a player controls in a D&D game. *My player character is an elf sorcerer and she's about thirty times cooler than I am.*

Roleplaying Game (RPG): A game in which the participants assume the roles of fictional characters in a story they create together. *I never thought I'd play a roleplaying game, but then I discovered DUNGEONS & DRAGONS.*

Roll up: Slang term meaning to create or build a character. *Hey Billy, want to get a bottle of Chianti and roll up some characters?*

Round: A measure of time completed when every character and creature has taken his or her turn in combat. *Protection from PMS only lasts one round, so you better get away from the Häagen-Dazs and peanut butter while you can.*

Spell: A single use, magical effect. *I'd like to cast a super-metabolism spell after eating all of the Häagen-Dazs and peanut butter.*

Total Party Kill (TPK): Slang term meaning when every character in a D&D campaign bites the dust. *After protection from PMS wore off, the DM sent our unsuspecting party into a dragon's lair and experienced his first-ever TPK.*

Undead: Dead monsters that just can't stay away from the living. *Call in the Ghostbusters. This is temple is chock full of undead creatures such as ghouls, vampires, and boomerang boyfriends.*

Endgame

Now that you've come to the end of this book, you may be asking yourself why exactly you read it. Maybe you're still not ready to jump into a game of D&D, or maybe you've already rolled up a bevy of characters you'll change out like your favorite handbags. Or maybe you're somewhere in the middle. Hopefully you at least have a better understanding of what exactly goes on in the basements, kitchens, and conference rooms of those who engage in a roleplaying game now and then.

People will look at you weird if you tell them you play D&D. They'll ask a lot of questions. They keep asking me when the novelty is going to wear off. How do I find time to keep playing? Why do I play? The answers are simple, really. The novelty won't wear off because every week is something new. How do I find time? When you're part of a group that depends on you, you make time. It's why people have personal trainers and seldom cancel first dates. *Why* I play should be obvious by now. I like the social aspect and the opportunity to tap into a side of myself once a week that would be inappropriate to tap into at the grocery store or in traffic. (Although I do find myself "puem pueming" cars that drive under the speed limit or pedestrians who don't wait for the walk symbol before they cross the street.) The question I get asked most often now is, will I continue to play? The answer? A resounding *yes*. For the first time in my life, I can honestly say I've got game.

At least on Mondays, I do.

ACKNOWLEDGEMENTS

The following people were kind enough to lend their wisdom, advice, time and opinions to the production of this book: Michele Carter, Randall Crews, Josh Fischer, Jodi Gross, Nina Hess, Karin Jaques, Mark Jessup, Desiree Jordan, Kristina Koser, Kim Lundstrom, Jodi Medlock, Kristina Morello, Christopher Perkins, Casey Reeter, Kate Ross, Ilja Rotelli, Liz Schuh, Bill Slavicsek, and Roxy Tobias.

Extra special thanks to the world's greatest party who have graciously and enthusiastically made this experience way more fun than imagined (and saved Astrid's life a few times in the process): Adam Colby, Linae Foster, Sara Girard, Elena Moye, Rich Redman, Scott Rouse, and Kevin Wilson.

In loving memory of Jak,
who bit it in battle shortly after
this book was written.
So I guess it was a trap, after all?